THE

SECULAR

CONGREGATION

THE
SECULAR
CONGREGATION

ROBERT A. RAINES

1817

HARPER & ROW, PUBLISHERS
NEW YORK, EVANSTON, AND LONDON

Grateful acknowledgment is made to the following for permission to reprint the copyrighted material listed below:

SYDNEY CARTER for excerpts from "Lord of the Dance" from Risk—New Hymns for a New Day, Vol. II, No. 3.

THE CHRISTIAN CENTURY FOUNDATION for excerpts from "Meditation for a Young Boy Confirmed" by Alan Paton. Copyright 1954 in the October 13, 1954 issue of The Christian Century. Used by permission of The Christian Century Foundation and Annie Laurie Williams, Inc.

HOLT, RINEHART AND WINSTON, INC. for excerpts from Are You Running with Me, Jesus? by Malcolm Boyd. Copyright © 1965 by Malcolm Boyd. Reprinted by permission of Holt, Rinehart and Winston, Inc.

THE VIKING PRESS, INC., THE MACMILLAN COMPANY OF CANADA, LTD., and MACMILLAN & CO. LTD., London, for "The Prayer of the Tortoise" from Prayers from the Ark by Carmen Bernos de Gasztold and translated by Rumer Godden. Copyright 1962 by Rumer Godden. Reprinted by permission of The Viking Press, Inc. and Macmillan & Co. Ltd.

K-T

LIBRARY OF CONGRESS CATALOG CARD NUMBER: 68-17584

To
the Congregation
of the
First Methodist Church
of
Germantown

PREFACE

The Voight Lectureship was established in honor of Bishop Edwin E. Voight when he retired as resident bishop of the Illinois Area of the Methodist Church. Bishop Voight is now serving as president of McKendree College. It was my privilege to give the first of this series of annual lectures in 1967 at McKendree College in Lebanon, Ill. I am grateful to the trustees of the lectureship and to Bishop Voight himself for their warm and gracious hospitality to me during those days. This book is the substance of those lectures.

I want also to thank the people of First Methodist Church of Germantown for their grace and patience in all that we have been through together in these recent years, and especially Ken Conners who has provided key leadership and constant encouragement in the guidance of both congregation and ministers.

I am in debt to all the ministers of the church, past and present, and in particular to the three men with whom I have been privileged to work during most of the years covered by this book. Ted Loder, my colleague in the co-ministry, has been responsible for a major part of whatever has been creative in our congregation; I have learned much from him, and we have found much together. Jerry Rardin blessed us all in these years with his rare capacity to understand and to encourage. Lawrence Curry, late and beloved minister of music of the church for more than thirty years, taught us as much about the ministry as about music.

I am grateful also to the loyal and forbearing office staff

and custodians of the church whose ministry to ministers as well as to congregation is constant.

Jennifer Allcock's courage and commitment have strengthened my faith. Joan Hemenway's creative insight and hope have encouraged me, and her painstaking editing of this manuscript substantially clarified and improved it. Virginia Hamilton once again has generously given her time, skill, and energy to the preparation of this manuscript, with humor and personal affirmation along the way.

Most of all, I am grateful to Peggy and the four children, who, albeit reluctantly, allow writing time to find a place in family vacations, and who cheerfully provide both the cost and the joy of the secular parsonage (next book).

August 15, 1967
Glen Arbor, Michigan

ROBERT A. RAINES

CONTENTS

THE
SECULAR
CONGREGATION

I

THE PIETIST-SECULARIST CONTROVERSY IN THE CONGREGATION

IN NOVEMBER, 1964, the First Methodist Church of Germantown suffered a financial crisis. Some church members refused to pledge to the coming year's budget, and we found ourselves far short of the needed funds. What brought on the crisis? It was the convergence of four controversial issues, telescoped into hot focus in the period of one month. The first issue was race. The clergy and many laymen had been actively working for the passage of the 1964 Civil Rights Bill—writing congressmen, circulating petitions, participating in prayer vigils. Some of our people resented this activity in addition to what they regarded as constant reference in sermons and prayers to racial incidents and issues. There was also the gradual appearance of more Negroes in the congregation.

The second issue was politics. That was the year of the Johnson-Goldwater presidential campaign. The clergy took positions on major election issues, which some members of the congregation thought tantamount to endorsing the Johnson-Humphrey ticket from the pulpit. A seminar on election issues was held in the church's social hall. Four local experts were invited to speak, on a nonpartisan basis, to these issues. While the four speakers tried to be nonpartisan in their comments, some of our people thought the evening had a distinctly anti-Goldwater flavor. We learned to our sorrow that it is not possible to have a nonpartisan seminar on hot political issues. A debate is more fair.

The third issue was sex. That October the church cele-

brated its second Arts Festival. One of the events was a per-
formance of Edward Albee's *The Zoo Story*[1] by the Union
Theological Seminary Players. Though the play was performed in the social hall and acted superbly, some of our
people found its language and sexual implications offensive.
They were appalled that the church should drag such sordid
dimensions of the world inside its own walls, corrupting our
youth and sullying ourselves.

The fourth issue was modern art. That was the year, only
the Lord knows why, that we decided upon a modernistic
design for our Finance Brochure. Some people were disturbed
by the artwork, which seemed to them grotesque. We learned
to our sorrow that it is unwise to attempt to communicate
with an entire congregation via unfamiliar art media without
considerable advance interpretation.

Granted that the emotional pitch in the nation was high
that fall. Granted that the clergy made mistakes of judgment,
diplomacy and interpretation. Granted that it was bad luck
that all this broke just before pledging time, though it often
seems to happen that way to us! Still, the basic issue under-
lying these circumstantial factors was this: Does the gospel of
Jesus Christ have to do with the real throbbing world where
people live—the world of race, sex, politics, modern art,
drama, poetry—or not? Ought the church of Christ to be
involved in the struggle for racial justice and peace and the
elimination of poverty, or not? Ought the church to expose its
people to the real, sordid world portrayed in *The Zoo Story*,
or not? Ought the church to listen to contemporary artists, the
secular prophets and spiritual alarm clocks of our day, or not?
Should sermons and prayers deal with the bitter anguished
world of power—black and white, East and West, North
Vietnamese and American—or not? Should the church seek
to change men's hearts only, and trust that they will then
"take" the gospel into the world to change it? Or should the
church seek also to change those political, economic, and so-

cial structures which condemn large numbers of Americans to poverty, ignorance, and disease, generation after generation?

This controversial question divides congregations across the country without regard to denomination or location. I have described the experience of the congregation I know best, not because it is extraordinary but precisely because it is typical. Father Kavanaugh in his book "A Modern Priest Looks at His Outdated Church poignantly puts his finger on the present controversy in American Roman Catholicism, and Rabbi Richard Rubenstein puts the Jewish dilemma in After Auschwitz.[2] It is this controversy which forces some ministers and priests and rabbis to leave their congregations, some to leave the ministry, some to be disciplined by their ecclesiastical superiors, some to acquiesce, some to compromise and struggle on. The controversy is heartrending, and sometimes churchrending. But I believe it to be necessary and potentially fruitful. In fact, where the church is not experiencing this controversy in some degree, it is slumbering through or trying to resign from the revolution in the modern world. The issue may be defined as the pietist-secularist controversy in the congregation. Let us first probe more deeply into the controversy itself and then see what can be done about it.

The Pietist-Secularist Controversy in the Congregation

The terms "pietist" and "secularist" shoot up red flags in the minds of many people. They are terms with negative connotations, popularly speaking, and therefore, if clearly defined, may help us to see the polarities involved more sharply. I should emphasize that I am not speaking here of pietism, which is a distortion, a sentimentalization, or an introversion of biblical piety. Nor am I speaking of secularism, which is the name for a godless ideology, a closed world-view operating very much like a religion without transcendence.

Some people regard "piety" as a matter of dubious devotions with an anti-this-world flavor. Other people regard "secularity" as having to do with that which is godless and materialistic. In fact, both terms are inherently neutral. "Piety is a style of response to God."[3] "Secularity"[4] is a style of participation in the history of the world. I grew up a pietist and am becoming a secularist. I try to keep one foot on each side of the river. As the gulf widens, it gets more and more painful.

Who is a pietist and who is a secularist? The *pietist* is church-centered. He looks for God primarily in the church, its Word and sacraments and communal life. He cites the priority that Jesus gave to loving God with all the heart, soul, mind, and strength (Mark 12:28-34).* He is more concerned that the essential faith be preserved than that it be relevant in the modern world. He insists that the church must not lose its savor (Matt. 5:13, KJV). He holds fast to the church at the risk of losing the world.

The *secularist* is world-centered. He looks for God primarily in the world, its words, events, and the communal life of the Nation and the nations. He cites the importance Jesus gave to loving the neighbor and quotes such passages as: "If any one says, 'I love God' and hates his brother, he is a liar . . ." (I John 4:20) and "So if you are offering your gift at the altar, and there remember that your brother has something against you, leave your gift there before the altar and go; first be reconciled to your brother, and then come and offer your gift" (Matt. 5:23-24). He is more concerned with the relevance of the gospel to the world than with its preservation. He holds fast to the world at the risk of losing the church.

The pietist thinks of God's action primarily in terms of the past. He wants continuity. His mood is nostalgia, his motto is, "Come weal or woe, the status quo!" He may emphasize an otherworldly Christianity. He thinks of sin as "private" im-

---

* Biblical references are to the Revised Standard Version of the Bible unless otherwise noted.

morality—stealing, lying, adultery—and of salvation in individualistic terms.

The secularist thinks of God's action primarily in terms of the future. He wants change. His mood is optimism, his motto is, "Come weal or woe, go-go-go!" He will emphasize a this-worldly Christianity. He thinks of sin as "public" immorality —injustice, prejudice, oppression—and of salvation in corporate terms (the nations are gathered before the king at the last judgment; Matt. 25:31 ff., italics added).

Both the pietist and the secularist say they want order and justice. But if they have to choose, the pietist will choose order because he abhors civil disobedience, and the secularist will choose justice because he abhors unjust laws. The pietist prays, "Lord, change me." The secularist prays, "Lord, change the world!" Presumably the reader has begun to locate himself in the controversy. One may find himself firmly entrenched on one side of the fence, or uncomfortably straddling the fence, or bouncing back and forth from one side to the other. In order more clearly to identify ourselves and our congregations, let us see how the pietist and secularist check out on such issues as the new theology, the new morality, Jesus Christ, and the Bible.

The New Theology

The pietist views the "death of God" theologians as heretics and/or atheists. The secularist, while denying that God is dead, may affirm that the imagery and language with which we have traditionally thought and spoken of God, are no longer meaningful to most modern men. Therefore, retranslation and reinterpretation of the doctrines of the church are needed. For example: Bishop John (*Honest to God*) Robinson preached a sermon on the ascension of Jesus at our church some years ago.[5] He spoofed a literal interpretation of the ascension by saying that if Jesus' physical body had indeed shot off into outer space, then Jesus was the first cosmonaut, and the difference between him and John Glenn was that Glenn got back. (It can be imagined how some of the congregation took that.) The bishop went on to interpret the ascension as not a matter of Jesus going literally *out* of this world, but of his being *over* this world as sovereign judge and redeemer. It was a thiswordly, instead of an otherwordly, understanding of the ascension. Many of our people found the sermon highly stimulating and provocative; others were offended. A poignant letter came the following week from a longtime member of the congregation who said, "If the Ascension, the Virgin Birth, the Immaculate Conception, the miracles, the Resurrection, etc. go down the drain, what's left of the faith?" That is, if one stone in the edifice of Christian doctrine is dislodged, won't the whole structure fall? Well, it may. Maybe it has to if the Christian faith is to be reformulated so that it may become believable in a secular era. I don't know. But I do know that while I do not happen to share the letter-writer's theological views, I can understand his feeling of insecurity at the questioning of a tenet of the faith he thought to be central.

Every pietist has his insecurity threshold. Mine is the resurrection. Once in a conversation in which my understanding of the resurrecton was rejected for one that I thought (and think) to be unbiblical, I found myself getting defensive and angry. Why? Later I realized that it was not so much that the resurrection was being questioned (it can take care of itself), but rather that my interpretation of it was brought into question. My security structure was shaken and I did not like the feeling. In a time of necessary theological questioning and reformulation, pietists will have to learn to live with uncongenial interpretations of major Christian doctrines without thinking furtive heretical thoughts about those who hold these interpretations.

At the same time they will, without apology, hold fast "the truth of the gospel" (Gal. 2:5, 14) as they are given to understand it. And they will caution secularists to be aware that in the valid attempt to reformulate Christian doctrine today, there is a high seduction quotient. It is the seduction of seeking to make Christianity (and Christians) intellectually acceptable to secular man. The Greeks are still seeking wisdom I Cor. 1:22). In a new preface to his book *The Spirit of Protestantism*,[6] Robert McAfee Brown writes:

The message of the gospel is not merely an italicized version of the message of the world. Nor is the task of Christians to whittle away their heritage until it is finally palatable to all. . . . There is a 'scandal' to the Christian faith, whether in its Protestant or Roman Catholic versions, and he who proclaims it, either through what he says or what he is or what he does, must be prepared to be called a fool for Christ's sake. The point must be stressed because much of what is going on at present on the Protestant scene gives the impression of being willing to jettison whatever is necessary in order to appeal to the modern mentality. But faith has never been easy, and if seeming irrelevance to the world is always the temptation of theological purists, undue accommodation to the world is equally destructive of faithful witness.

The trouble is, it is not always easy to tell whether you or somebody else is being a fool for Christ's sake or just a damn fool.

The New Morality

The secularist thinks of morality in terms of context rather than content. He speaks of only one commandment, the commandment to love, and stresses Christian freedom to love the neighbor in the spontaneity of the spirit. He "loves" to quote Augustine, "Love God and do as you please," and Luther "Trust God and sin on bravely," declaring that love can never know ahead of time what its imperatives will be in a given situation. The pietist thinks of morality in terms of content rather than context. He speaks of many commandments, laws, and rules, and he stresses Christian responsibility to obey them. He loves to talk about "the narrow gate" (Matt. 7:13) and "the house built on rock" (Matt. 7:24). And sometimes he alleges that the secularist conveniently forgets the first parts of Augustine and Luther's admonitions, simply "doing as he pleases and sinning on bravely."

One example of the conflict between the "old" morality and the "new" morality happened in our congregation recently. One of our able young men graduating from Union Theological Seminary was rejected for the Methodist ministry by the Philadelphia Conference Board of Ministerial Training. The reason was that he refused to promise that he would not smoke or drink—a rule in the *Discipline* of the Methodist Church which applies to its candidates for the ministry, though not, significantly, to its candidates for membership in the congregation. (Such a rule would vastly decrease both Methodist members and money.) It can be argued that the Board of Ministerial Training had no choice but to reject the young man because, after all, the rule was still on the books. It can also be argued that it is contrary to the New Testament to assign one morality to ministers of the church and another to members of the church, that if we want to get literal about it, there is more New Testament support for an ethic of pacifism than there is for abstinence, and that it is as unbiblical to tie abstinence to the Methodist ministry as it is to tie celibacy to the Roman Catholic priesthood. All these ethical issues are matters for individual vocation, not ecclesiastical legislation. In any case, the matter was brought to our Official Board, where it was voted nearly unanimously to memorialize the General Conference, the quadrennial policy-making body of the Methodist Church, to eliminate this rule as inconsistent with New Testament teaching regarding the responsible freedom of the Christian man.

Another painful example of the breakdown of the "old" morality has to do with sex ethics for the young unmarried. In this issue the pietist has one response, with varying degrees of conviction or despair: "Thou shalt not." The secularist points out that biblical and church directives are just not being taken seriously by modern youth, that "naughty-naughty" is no longer (if it ever was) an adequate sex ethic, and that it is a long jump from the age of the chastity belt to that of the pill. He declares that the church has to deal with the real *Playboy-Virginia Woolf*, back-seat-of-the-car world in which young people live today, and that the teaching of the church must not consist in legalistic "do's" and "don'ts," but should enable its youth to act responsibly in each situation, discerning what is best for the personhood of the other. The pietist may acknowledge much of this, but goes on to ask, "What is a responsible sex ethic which in fact is something more than 'relax and enjoy it'?" or "Do you really expect a teen-ager with a girl in his arms in the back seat of his car or on the couch in her parlor to ponder what is best for personhood?"

Jesus Christ

The secularist is fascinated by the humanity of Jesus. He identifies with the temptations, loneliness, and conflicts of Jesus. He is moved by the Gethsemane anguish and the cry of desolation from the cross. Albert Camus's leading character in *The Fall* says of Jesus, "He cried aloud his agony and that's why I love him, my friend who died without knowing."[7] He delights in a Jesus whose wholehearted celebrations drew snide remarks from his enemies to the effect that he ate and drank too much and associated with disreputable people (Matt. 11:19). He is impressed by a Jesus who started a riot in the cathedral church of the nation (Mark 11:15-18), and shook the religious establishment to its foundations. He explains away the miracles or ignores them as not meaningful. For him, to be a Christian is to be a man.

The pietist is committed to the mystery of Jesus. He believes that Jesus is something more than an example or a

friend at a party or on the picket line. Teilhard de Chardin
wrote:

Some think to make you more lovable in my eyes by praising
almost exclusively the charm and the kindness of your human face
as men saw it long ago on earth But if I sought only a human
being to cherish, would I not turn to those whom you have given
me here and now in all the charm of their flowering? Do we not all
have around us irresistibly lovable mothers, brothers, sisters,
friends? Why should we go searching the Judea of two thousand
years ago? No, what I cry out for, like every other creature, with
my whole being, and even with all my passionate earthly longings,
is something very different from an equal to cherish: It is a God to
adore.[8]

The pietist believes that God was doing a unique thing in the
life, death, and resurrection of Jesus, and that he is called to
obey Jesus as the authority of his life and to trust in him as the
one who heals and forgives by the power of God. The pietist
holds that the miracles, however we understand them or fail
to understand them, are an essential dimension of the mystery
of Jesus. For him, to be a Christian is to be in Christ.

Many of our children are secularists, and most of our
grandchildren will be. I remember years ago reading a Bible
story book about Jesus to my then nine-year-old daughter. I
could almost see her skeptical eyebrows lifting as miracle
after miracle was read to her, and Jesus was presented as a
man literally "out of this world." Years later she heard a
young minister describing his work in Appalachia among the
poor, and she found *this* idea of what it means to follow Jesus,
and what sort of person Jesus was, compelling. She was not
and is not attracted by his halo, but she is attracted by his
humanity.

In one of our *koinonia* groups the book *Jesus Of Nazareth*[9] was studied. Some people were appalled at the questions
raised in the book about the authenticity of some of the gospel
incidents and of some of the words of Jesus. Others were

grateful for a book which sought to separate myth, legend, and fact, and thus for the chance to believe in Jesus without a halo.

So we struggle in the congregation, while getting rid of the halo and affirming the humanity of Jesus, to acknowledge his mystery.

The Bible

If the Bible is the Word of God in the words of men, the pietist will come down hard on the Word of God and the secularist on the words of men. The pietist affirms that the Bible is the normative touchstone of the faith and life of the church. He has more confidence in God's revelation in ancient history (the Bible) than in modern history (contemporary events). For example, on the issue of particular or universal salvation, the pietist notes that the weight of biblical evidence is on the side of the particular or special salvation of some men, but not all men. Thus, regardless of his intuition that the father of the prodigal and elder sons will eventually win over the elder son (Luke 15:11-32), he feels obligated to espouse a particularist position. The secularist, however, insists that the Bible is not to be regarded as "law" for Christians seeking solutions to theological and moral problems today. He believes that the Bible is not to be consulted as infallible oracle but as a unique, though not exclusive, source of insight and power. He points out that the Spirit did not stop speaking to the church when the pages of the Bible were written. He will note here and there in the Bible hints and hopes of universal salvation (e.g., I Tim. 4:10; Rom. 11:32). Indeed, he will note the hope that not only all human beings but the whole creation will be saved (Rom. 8:18 ff.). He will trust his own intuition, growing out of his sense of solidarity with all men, that all men shall be saved, as the Spirit's gift to our time. He will exercise his biblical freedom to take its hint in that direction. For him the Bible is not a closed but an open book. The pietist replies that all too quickly we make the Bible say what we want it to say or ignore it when its testimony is contrary to our opinion or the prevailing cultural mood.

Who are you—a pietist, or a secularist, or a bit of both? I believe that the pietist and the secularist need each other and that each provides a necessary corrective to the other. The pietist accuses the secularist of trying to be "worldlier than thou," and warns him not to confuse holy worldliness[10] with just plain worldliness.[11] The secularist accuses the pietist of trying to be "holier-than-thou", and warns him not to confuse worldly holiness[12] with otherwordly holiness.[13] The secularist knows that it is possible for a man to be "converted to Christ" while remaining unconverted to Christ's ministry in the world, blind to his responsibility to participate in Christ's sufferings in the sufferings of mankind. The pietist knows that it is possible for a man to be "converted to the world," sharing in its sufferings valiantly, while remaining unconverted to Christ, blind to his need to participate in Christ's life in the Word and sacraments of his church. He knows that salt can lose its savor, that light can shade imperceptibly into the shadows and eventually disappear, that leaven can lose its identity and thus its vocation in the lump. As John Carr puts it, "To be truly pious is to be thoroughly secular, and to be truly secular is to be thoroughly pious."

So much for a thumbnail sketch of the pietist-secularist controversy. What can we do about it? How can the tension be made creative instead of destructive?

A Critical Task of Every Congregation Today Is to Keep the Pietist and the Secularist within Hearing Distance of Each Other and to Reconcile Them

The co-ministry structure of our clergy team has enabled our people to "hear" both pietist and secularist emphases.

While Ted Loder, my colleague in the co-ministry, and I share a basic theological compatibility, we relate to each other as pietist and secularist. I am the pietist, he the secularist. Sunday after Sunday the theological viewpoints of each of us are exposed to scrutiny by the other and by the entire congregation. Neither of us can get away with anything. Both of us have constantly to rethink and rework our own thought in response to the thought of the other and the congregation. The result is not that either converts the other to his position but, rather, that each comes to recognize the partiality of his own view of the truth, and to respect the truth his colleague sees. Because Ted and I are living and working through the pietist-secularist tension ourselves, the congregation shares the same struggle for truth along with us.

It takes a mature congregation to sustain theological diversity in its ministers and among its people without yielding either to confusion or to polarization. But where everybody concerned can stand the heat, it can be a remarkably creative and productive experience. We all learn that our theology has been partially shaped by our psychology, and that what we want to believe or have to believe, we find ways of believing. We learn about forgiveness and mutual forbearance. Either we learn or we blow apart.

It is my conviction that any team or staff ministry should try to have the pietist and secularist viewpoints represented among its ministers. A congregation with one minister should encourage lay expressions of views different from those of the minister (as well as similar to his) in sermon, prayer, and lecture. Every congregation must learn in its own experience that it is not a matter of eliminating either pietist or secularist, but of listening to both. A friend put it vividly in a letter: "I would hope that we could keep both the baby and the bathwater, doing community organization in slum areas, and in that context developing depth relationships between people, fighting our [Philadelphia] corrupt magistrates' system, and living the life of prayer that will enable us to fight with love towards the magistrates and bosses who support them, trying to renew the public structures, and being a sign of the kingdom to our neighbor. I cannot believe that the picketers and the pray-ers must forever go their separate ways."

Nor can I. God is surely calling all of us, pray-ers and picketers, to grope our way toward a secular piety which will be both relevant to this world and faithful to Jesus Christ.

A Secular Piety Will Affirm with the Secularist the Secularization of the World and the Church as the Work of God

What is secularization? In *The Secular City*[14] Harvey Cox writes:

> Secularization is man turning his attention away from worlds beyond, and towards this world and this time. . . . Pluralism and tolerance are the children of secularization. They represent a society's unwillingness to enforce any particular world-view on its citizens. [Hence the Supreme Court's decisions on Bible reading and prayer in the public schools.] When a school or hospital passes from ecclesiastical to public administration, the procedure is called secularization. . . .

Contemporary theology is pointing out in a convincing way that God is at work here and now in this world, and that history, i.e. social change, is precisely his arena of action. The striking fact is that this very insight is a biblical one.[15] The God who is bringing in the secular era today is the God of Abraham forever calling his people to leave their cherished ways and venture forth into an unknown future (Gen. 12 ff.; Heb. 11:8).[16] He is the God of Moses always seeking to liberate the captives of the world (Exod. 3:7-10). (It is with this Exodus God that Jesus identified his own ministry, Luke 4:18.) He is the Easter God of Jesus powering the revolutionary and reforming thrust of our own time and world, working to bring racial justice and international peace and health to all mankind. We need not fear secularization but can rejoice in it as not only our destiny but God's providence.

Yet secularization is painful. It is painful for us to realize that the world, not the church, is the center of God's concern. It is painful to realize that God is not pro-Christian but pro-people, that God does not love capitalist beings or communist beings but *human* beings, that it is not the vocation of the church to run the world but, rather, to serve it (Mark 10:35-44).

It is painful to have familiar and beloved customs changed. A layman of our congregation once said to me, "This isn't the same congregation I joined thirty-one years ago." And he is right. It isn't. There's a *world* of difference. There is in each of us, on some occasions and in some matters, a "stop the world, I want to get off" reaction to change. At the same time we realize that if the congregation does not adapt its language and life to changing social circumstances, it will rapidly find itself swept aside by the tides of history. A friend said that when he returned to his hometown, after being away for several years, everything in the city had changed but the churches! That comment was not a eulogy but an epitaph. Secularization is painful. But secularization is also liberating.

It frees us from our provincialisms. It frees us to be genuinely at ease with people whose belief and behavior are different from our own (and without self-righteousness or condemnation). It frees us of our presumptuous idea that the world is waiting for us to tell it what to think and how to live. It frees us from any "where will you spend eternity?" strain that survives in us. It frees us to become a *congregation without walls*[17]—theological walls, denominational walls, moralistic walls, institutional walls. In Chapters II and III we shall explore how a congregation begins to take down its walls. But now let us hear the secularist reminding us that we can trust the God who is bringing in the future.

A Secular Piety Will Affirm with the Pietist the Tradition of the Church as the Work of God

The tradition is the faith which has been handed down to us: "For I delivered to you as of first importance what I also received . . ." (I Cor. 15:3). To affirm the essential tradition of the church does not mean fearfully to hold onto language and forms which time shows to be obsolete. It does mean to affirm that God was alive yesterday as he is today. He is the God of Abraham, of Moses, and of Jesus, the God who has made us his people and given us the Scriptures, the sacraments, the covenant. We do not come *de novo* into the secular era, but surrounded and preceded by a cloud of witnesses. We stand on the shoulders of men who struggled to be faithful to God before us, whose children we are. Acknowledgment of the essential tradition is not optional but the precondition of discovering our own identity and vocation under God in our day. We shall not discern where we are going except as we remember where we have been. The church lives by both hope and memory. As we take the future seriously, so must we take the past seriously. This came home to me some time ago during a week-long conference of twenty Roman Catholic and Protestant clergy discussing and sharing "the Spiritual Life." The conference was held in St. John's Abbey, a Benedictine monastery in Collegeville, Minnesota. We rose for Mass, concelebrated every morning at seven, shared meals, read papers, discussed ideas, established friendships, and concluded each day with a brief service of evening prayer led by one of the Protestants.

Strangely, I found myself more grateful than I had been for our Protestant heritage. Professor Horton Davies of Princeton University gave a paper entitled *"The Puritan and Pietist Traditions of Protestant Spirituality."*[18] Here were the seventeenth-century Puritans whom we caricature as mean, self-righteous killjoys (and doubtless some of them were). But these were men who believed in the absolute sovereignty and holiness of almighty God, men who revered the Bible as the normative witness to God's Word, gave it priority in their worship, and studied it with a rigor and devotion to which most contemporary Christians are strangers. These were men who believed in loving God with the mind and who founded most of the early universities in America for the purpose of educating their clergy. It ill becomes us, a people flabby in the capacity for self-discipline, averse to intellectual rigor, and adrift on a sea of pseudo-freedom which much of the time is an aimless amorality (T. S. Eliot once said, "We are not emancipated; we are just unbuttoned"), to castigate the Puritans. We may deride their vices, but God knows how desperately we lack their virtues!

And here were the eighteenth-century pietists—the Moravians and Anabaptists in Germany, the Methodists and Baptists in England and America—men regarded as enthusiastic fools by the sophisticates of their time (and doubtless some of them were). But these were men who sought the purpose of God in Bible study and prayer with a passion of which we are ignorant. These were men who involved themselves in the sufferings of the lowest economic and social classes which were scorned by the established church. The Wesleyan movement in England[19] reminds us that genuine social reformation can begin with the change of men's hearts just as surely as it can begin with the change of a society's laws. Indeed, unless both are changed, there can be no deep and lasting reformation.

I found myself more grateful that I had been earlier for our Roman Catholic heritage. I was amazed at the caliber of the young men who are giving themselves to a life of celibacy, poverty, and obedience in this secular era (though they are struggling with the tensions and frustrations of monastic life in such an era). They know something about personal consecration of which our hedonistic culture has divested most of us. The Benedictines have been a going concern for fourteen hundred years. They have a sense of history which allows them to participate in today's revolution without losing their bearings.

That conference helped me realize in a new way the importance of knowing where we come from. We are given our identity and thus our vocation not only from the future but also, and indispensably, from the past. Today's faithful congregation will be a *congregation with roots*—theological, denominational, ethical, institutional—a congregation not bound to its past, but with respect for it. In Chapters IV and V we shall explore how a congregation seeks to find and live by its roots. But now let us hear the pietist remind us that we can trust the God who brought in the past.

A Critical Task of Every Congregation Today is to Keep the Pietist and the Secularist within Hearing Distance of Each Other, and to Reconcile Them

Such reconciliation will not require or produce uniformity of opinion, but will seek to enable people to speak the truth as they see it, to listen to each other, not regarding those who differ from them as either knaves or fools but as men of good will who differ, but who will not let their differences alienate them. John Harmon writes, "No significant change will occur in our urban ministries without controversy, because the issues involved are so deep. . . . controversy is hard for us to bear. . . . But if the churches cannot bear controversy, who can? We are the people who know that men are held together by God and not by any timid human concensus."[20]

We have been learning in our own congregational experience the truth of those words. We believe that the congregation must embrace the partisans of right and left, holding within its fellowship the antagonisms of the world and by grace transforming them into creative polarities. For the congregation is the body of Christ, where our diversities need not tear us apart, but can enrich us, humble us, and lead us to deeper unity than we have known.

During the pledge crisis of our congregation in November, 1964, the pastors put aside other obligations and began to go into the homes of those who felt alienated from us or from the congregation. We listened, night after night, in home after home. We listened and we learned how we had failed to interpret what we were trying to do, and how we had offended when it had not been necessary. We found in some instances basic difference of opinion as to the proper mission of our congregation. We sought to reconcile and to be reconciled. In January the Finance Commission of the congregation met to decide what to do. The ministers were willing to take the licking without comment, to cut back on program, pull in their belts and do the best they could. But the lay leader of the congregation reported that one young family, already giving a substantial pledge to the church, wanted to take on an additional pledge, one of the large ones not remade for the coming year, to help maintain the church program. He also read a letter from a man in the community who was not a member of the congregation. The man wrote that he believed the program of the congregation to be of great importance to the whole renewal effort in Germantown, and that therefore the church program must not be cut back one iota. He enclosed a substantial check and stated that he hoped there would be many other such checks to make up the full budget. The meeting broke when the president of the Board of Trustees said, "This congregation has never failed to meet its responsibilities. Let's go back to our people and ask them to increase their pledges enough to underwrite the full program of the church. And let's begin by increasing our pledges!"

So we asked our people to repledge. Some who had not pledged before, now did; many increased their pledges, some

doubled and even tripled theirs. The budget was oversub-
scribed. For our congregation, it was a turning point.

These are hard days for both laymen and clergy in the
church. Laymen may feel that they joined the church under
one set of rules, and now, in the middle of the game, some
long-hair cleric hardly out of seminary starts changing the
rules. Clergy, in a church like the one I serve at least, may
find themselves in a human tug-of-war, with young whippersnappers pulling from the left and old codgers pulling from
the right. And it is not entirely a matter of age. I know some
very young codgers and some very old whippersnappers! The
clergy are in a situation reminiscent of "The Charge of the
Light Brigade":

> Codgers to the right of them.
> Whippersnappers to the left of them.
> Codgers and whippersnappers in front of them.
> Into the jaws of death,
> Into the mouth of Hell,
> Ride the clergy!

Here is the pastor's anguish. The pastor has a dual calling.
On the one hand, he is to *lead* the sheep, speaking the Word
to his people in a prophetic ministry. And on the hand
he is to *gather* the sheep, not losing one of them in a pastoral
ministry. But he may find that one phrase in a sermon or one
action which he feels to be inherent in his prophetic ministry
disrupts, and in some cases destroys, his pastoral ministry.
"You always hurt the one you love" is not only the title of a
song but a fact of life for many a clergyman and many a
layman today. Some of the saddest moments in my ministry
have come when I alienated someone I care about by something I said or did—sometimes unnecessarily or injudiciously,
and sometimes unavoidably. Conversely, some of the most
joyous moments have come when an alienated one and I have
together heard a reconciling Word. It is a great gift to dis-

cover that you can love a man with whom you violently dis-
agree on a matter important to you both. I don't believe a
pastor should work only with those who see things his way,
and to heaven with the rest. We've got the Moses-misery;
we've got to get the whole crowd to the Promised Land, and
not just a bunch of commandos in the crowd (though the
commandos may turn out to be prophets and not just pests).
Perhaps that reconciliation to God, to one another, and to
ourselves, will come only at the foot of a very controversial
Cross.

One evening while at the Benedictine Monastery in Collegeville, Minnesota, I entered the sanctuary at night. It has a
beautiful architectural design with high, vaulted ceiling, a
large marble altar toward the front, over which was suspended a huge cross. Behind the altar were the choir stalls. I
walked up front, knelt down at the left of the sanctuary, and
looked up at the cross. I saw that there were five circles on the
cross—at the head and the foot, on the two sides, and in the
middle. And as I looked, I realized that these circles represented the wounds of Christ—the crown of thorns, the nails in
the hands and feet, and the spear in the side. As I looked at
these symbolic wounds, I began to think about the wounds in
my life and the wounds in the lives of people I know and the
wounds of the world. Suddenly I was startled to see the face
of Christ looking at me through the circle at the head of the
cross. For a moment I was amazed. Then I realized that on
the other side of the cross, visible to the choir, was the crucifix. It struck me in a fresh way that Christ is joined to us
precisely in our wounds and in the wounds of the world, and
that we find Him there, in suffering to bring us joy, and in
controversy, reconciliation.

SECULAR EVANGELISM: Covenant House

How does a congregation take its walls down?
How does a congregation "go secular"?
Herewith a parable.

IN MAY, 1963, the civil rights demonstrations exploded in Birmingham, Alabama. The next week, the Rev. Andrew Young, Martin Luther King's right-hand man in the Southern Christian Leadership Conference, was invited by a group of Germantown residents to address a public rally in our sanctuary on what was happening in Birmingham. In the diverse crowd that gathered that night, many of whom had no relation to our church, and some of whom were not Christian, were two young women. One was Joan Hemenway, at that time Associate Editor of *Youth Magazine* (United Church of Christ), who came to cover the event for her magazine. She brought with her a friend, Jennifer Allcock, an English doctor in the United States for a year of pediatric training. Neither woman had ever been to First Methodist; neither had a significant relation to any congregation at the time. Jennifer, in fact, was hostile to the institutional church she had known in England. But they were intrigued that a church would hold a civil rights rally in its sanctuary. So they came back on Sunday mornings for a few weeks to see what made us tick. In the following months they were drawn deeply into the life of the church, and in December of that year became members, though both of them thought they would be gone from Philadelphia within six months. Jennifer was considering an offer to teach medicine in a Nigerian hospital, and Joan had made application to the Peace Corps.

However, they found themselves discussing with friends in the church the possibility of engaging in some form of mission in the Wister area of Germantown. Germantown is an urban section of the city of Philadelphia, and Wister is one of its most depressed areas. At the time the women were living in a lovely suburban home. The wild idea came to them of renting an apartment in the Wister area in the hope of helping to serve whatever human needs should manifest themselves Jennifer had long dreamed of some day starting a medical practice in such a poverty area.

Things jelled in March, 1964, when both turned down their opportunities to serve abroad and, with eight other people, committed themselves to seek some form of mission in Wister. We convenanted together to search for the shape and substance of the mission to which God would call us by committing ourselves to daily prayer and Bible study, and by meeting weekly to share insights and make decisions. At the second meeting Joan jolted the group. She had been talking with a friend about the apartment idea. The friend said, "You shouldn't rent. If you really mean business and aren't just going there to look around, you should buy a house and put your roots down." Joan said, "That would be great but we don't have any money." Her friend replied, "I'll loan you five thousand dollars."

We felt we were not likely to get more convincing leading from the Lord than that! So that night the ten of us decided to borrow the money and start looking for a house to buy. The idea was that the two women would move into such a house, while the rest of us would support the venture with money, time, and concern—everything short of actual residence. (See Chapter IV for a full description of the commitments of this group which came to be known as the Covenant Group.)

Within two months we had found a house that seemed admirably suited to our purposes. The block was about 60 per cent Negro. The house had a kitchen and bathroom on the second floor, making it readily convertible into an apartment for the women. Downstairs there was a large living room suitable for activities of all kinds, a kitchen, a bathroom, and a dining room. The house was in poor condition but nonetheless, was selling for $4,500.00. We bought it. It came to be called Covenant House.

That summer was spent converting the house into a decent place to live. One Saturday morning a white woman, who lived a few houses down the block, knocked on the door. My wife, who was in the vestibule sanding the baseboard, invited the woman to come in. She did so, and came directly to the point. "Is it true that two white girls have bought this house and are going to live here?"

"Yes," answered my wife.

"Why?" asked the woman.

"Well, they wanted to live in an integrated area, and one of them who is a doctor hopes someday to start a medical practice here in the house." The woman shook her head in amazement and said, "My God, I can't believe it! Maybe this neighborhood's got a chance after all. I've gotta go home and make myself a highball!"

The question was first raised, "Why are you here?" The Covenant House Newsletter of February, 1965, put it this way.

The answer to this question is always different—and difficult. Among ourselves and other committed Christians from our own milieu we may begin to talk about reconciliation, the search for new meanings in Christian neighborliness, the call of Christ which sends each of us into the world, or the attempt simply to live out the courage to be. But among the people on Bringhurst Street we are at a loss for an answer. To specifically identify ourselves as Christians called to be in the world opens up the doors to misconceptions and prejudices about the Church and religion and ourselves, and may close many doors which might lead to new relationships. . . . When the world of today seems to be calling for "incognito" Christians, how do we proclaim the good news of the Gospel?

On August 1, 1964, Joan and Jennifer moved into the house on Bringhurst Street. We wanted them to have plenty of time to establish a natural neighbor presence on the block. We did not want the house to be wrongly identified as the outpost of a church or social agency. We agreed that no programs of service were to be started for at least a year. It was to be a year of incognito presence, an "apostolate of being there."

During those first months children on the block flocked into the house and yard. Informal "clubs" came into being on the initiative of the children; some tutoring began, and a number of parties were held for children and with families on the block. Jennifer and Joan identified themselves with the local neighborhood council. They began to become neighbors in the neighborhood. The response to Covenant House took us completely by surprise. Almost fifty-seven varieties of Protestants, many Roman Catholics and non-Christians helped us paint, plaster, and repair the house, in addition to giving money. We spent $5,000.00 that first year, beginning to repay the loan and making major renovations on the house. $3000 was provided by members of the Covenant Group, $2,000.00 was given by others interested in the project. Jennifer wrote a letter, describing the venture, to a Roman Catholic friend who is a teacher. Her friend wrote back, "I am excited about what you are doing and would like to have a small part in it." In the letter was a check for $50.00 and every month thereafter came a check for $50.00 from this friend. Sometime later the friend decided to go to graduate school. Jennifer wrote her saying how grateful we all were for her generous help in the critical early months of the venture and that we realized that her new study program would make it impossible for her to continue helping financially. A letter came back from her friend with a check for $800.00 enclosed and the word, "This will keep me up to date until the fall of 1967." Gulp! Through the years we have been blessed and encouraged by people giving themselves and their gifts in utterly unanticipated and generous ways. There are times when we sense the Holy Spirit moving in our midst, and we are filled with wonder.

The hope of all of us in the early months was expressed in a newsletter to interested friends, dated September, 1964. "This first newsletter is trying to say that we are deeply aware that you too are with us. . . . We are strengthened by the intermeshing of this knowledge with such words from the Gospel as these: 'Thus says the Lord of Hosts, the God of Israel, to all the exiles whom I have sent into exile from Jerusalem to Babylon: Build houses and live in them; plant gardens and eat their produce. . . . seek the welfare of the city where I have sent you into exile, and pray to the Lord on its behalf, for in its welfare you will find your welfare' (Jer. 29:4, 5, 7)." That first year saw the secular presence of the church quietly "happening" on Bringhurst Street as we searched for a style of being, doing, and saying which would effectively communicate the gospel in that place.

If the first year was an apostolate of *being* there, the second was an apostolate of *doing* there. Myriad needs quickly became manifest and we became impatient to start trying to meet them. The first programed venture was a nursery school for children on the block in the summer of 1965. It was highly successful and has since become a year-round school with two competent paid teachers, one of them a mother in the neighborhood. The school is fully accredited by the state, and has served over thirty children on the immediate block in the last two years. When the Federal Get Set program was inaugurated, we thought that our school would become superfluous.

But not so. We discovered that many three- and four-year-olds of working mothers simply could not cross busy city streets to get to and from a Get Set school located several blocks from their homes. In addition, children of families whose annual income was as little as $50.00 above the maximum annual income allowed, were not eligible. And on top of that, it is estimated, certainly borne out by our own experience, that Get Set covers only 60 per cent of the children needing such schooling. So our nursery school continues to serve children on the block, many of whose older brothers and sisters are involved in the life of Covenant House in other ways. Because the school is in a house on the block, the youngsters are literally "at home" there. They know they are welcome and that they belong. We believe that their capacity for and interest in learning are significantly enhanced by their "at home" security.

A full-scale tutoring program started in the fall of 1965. Approximately twenty adults and twice as many children have participated in the last two years. The tutors come from many denominational backgrounds. Among them was a Roman Catholic priest, who came every Wednesday night to tutor a child in mathematics. The following year, three high school girls from a neighboring Roman Catholic preparatory school came, complete with nun, to tutor. They are doing a most creative job. For more than a year we have had the excellent help of a remedial reading expert who has been testing the children and teaching the tutors. In addition to evidence of some improvement in school, personal relationships between tutor and child, and the child's family, have in many instances become very meaningful. A library was started in the house in conjunction with the tutoring program so that youngsters could have a convenient time and place for guided reading as well as books which could help them to understand their urban environment. The August, 1965, Covenant House *Newsletter* described it.

Every Wednesday afternoon we arrive home to find groups of children and adults in twos and threes all over the house, their heads close together assiduously concentrating on *The Bank Street Readers* (Macmillan Co.). We have discovered that the children are highly motivated to learn, but sadly lacking in tools with which to work: a third-grader who should be in fifth cannot yet read at all; a fifth-grader was recently proud to have completed the second-grade-level book.

In October of that second year, 1965, Jennifer started her medical practice. At first it was primarily a pediatric practice, but because there is no other doctor in the immediate vicinity, the service soon broadened to encompass the needs of families. It is a genuine neighborhood General Practice of the kind one seldom sees today. The 1966 winter *Newsletter* described how the medical practice opened doors to other personal ministries.

The mother of one of the first pediatric patients is now providing us with part-time cleaning services. The husband in another family recently returned from two years in jail. We put him in touch with *Opportunities Industrialization* and last week he began training which will ultimately make him employable. A third family, having serious marital problems and temporarily estranged, had sufficient trust to use Jennifer as an intermediary in communicating with each other and with their lawyer, as well as checking on the welfare of their children. They have since entered into marriage counseling. It is encouraging that the medical practice provides opportunity for real communication with the white families on the street, a few of whom, having been hostile in the past, now express their appreciation for the presence of a doctor on the street.

In the first two years of the practice more than one hundred families in the neighborhood were served.

Jennifer teaches part time in a medical college to earn her living, so that she can charge minimal fees for the neighborhood practice. But she does charge, so that people have the dignity and the responsibility of paying something for the service. One day a mother brought a small child to the office. The child's arm was swollen, and black and blue. Whatever had bruised the arm had happened, obviously, a day or more before. Jennifer asked the mother what had happened, and the mother replied that the child had fallen off a table. "Why," demanded Jennifer, "didn't you bring the baby in right away?" The mother said, "I didn't have the money then." Jennifer assured her that next time she must come right away, even without the money, and that she could pay later.

In such poignant ways we discover that poor people learn by bitter experience that they usually have to have money before they can be admitted to a clinic or a hospital. There is still in this country an unholy (and largely unconscious) alliance between money and medicine—the more money you have the better medicine you can buy. Few, if any, of the preschool children on the block, for example, have ever been to a dentist. While many doctors and dentists give hours to charity work in hospitals, few are willing or able to serve the poor directly where they live. Doctors and dentists just don't open offices on streets like Bringhurst. For over one hundred years we have sent medical missionaries abroad. Isn't it time we support such work in the urban slums of the richest country in the history of the world?

During the third year of the Covenant House ministry, one of our group members began teaching in the Wister Elementary School. Her exposure to the community from that perspective enlarged our understanding of the complex needs and problems of the area, and of the huge job faced by a school in such an area. That same year two social workers began to give half a day a week to counsel with people whose needs were being uncovered in the medical and educational ministries of the House. Our ideas of people on welfare began to change radically as we came to know some personally. Here, for example, was a mother with eight children, trying to

raise, feed, house, clothe, and care for her children on a welfare check of about $45.00 a week supplemented by a check,
usually delinquent, from her absentee husband. When the
money runs out and the gas is turned off and there is no
food to put in the children's stomachs, no shoes without holes
to put on their feet, what does such a mother do?

How many times at a backyard barbecue over steak, or in a
country club over martini and shrimp, or in a church Board
Room over well-polished mahogany, does one hear someone
say, "These welfare people are irresponsible, dirty, and immoral. Why don't they pay their bills; why can't they pull
themselves up by their bootstraps the way I did. All this
money to keep them going is draining us dry. Most of them
could get jobs if they were willing to work." Contrary to un-
founded popular opinion, "Less than 1% of the 7.3 million
Americans on public welfare are capable of getting off the
relief rolls and going to work," according to a recent government analysis made by Joseph A. Califano, Jr., generally
regarded as President Johnson's top aide on domestic matters.
. . .[1] Welfare people are just statistics until you know some
of them personally, and you cannot *know* them until you are
there *with* them. This mother with her eight children is cour-
ageously trying to raise her family under conditions that
would drive many of us middle-class types to drink or to the
psychiatrist, but she has neither time, energy, nor money for
either. She lives with a power and hope that shame us who
know her.

The summer of 1967 found over fifty children on the block
going to camps, one of which was a special program called
"Spark." Organized by a suburban congregation it involved
twenty-five neighborhood children in a creative approach to
language and arts combined with fun and games. Suburban
people and congregations are finding Covenant House a way
into urban need, a small but concrete way to bridge the gap
between human need and human resources.

The summer of 1967 saw the launching of a Family Planning Clinic. Several years before, Planned Parenthood wanted to set up an office in the Germantown community, but there was too much opposition from local Roman Catholics and some Negro Protestant clergymen. Jennifer had long desired to make available this kind of service so desperately needed in the Wister area. As has happened to us so often, a way and a person just appeared. A young gynecologist living in Germantown, hearing about Jennifer and Covenant House, offered his services to start such a clinic. Foundation help was secured, a registered nurse and receptionist volunteered their services, and the clinic got under way two nights monthly (soon becoming one night a week). Information is given, fittings are made, pills and devices are dispensed. Very few of the women being served would ever have found their way to a private doctor or a public clinic, expecially when the latter are open only during traditional working hours.

A recent *Newsletter* sums up some of our dilemmas and breakthroughs in the daily person-to-person ministry of Covenant House.

Ordinarily we prefer to play the role of neighbor rather than Lady Bountiful: to give advice only when asked and to give direct assistance only in ways that will enhance the independence and self-respect of our friends on the block. For instance, when one mother found herself unable to purchase the required minimum of food stamps, we loaned her money—and she has repaid us by cleaning the nursery and the office. A freezer and refrigerator donated to the House were passed on to two large families who are now better equipped to plan shopping trips around special sales. On another occasion, when our help with a letter to a landlord proved inadequate, one of the Covenant House men accompanied the bewildered tenant to the rental office where his silent support prompted the writing of a fair lease. Much of our help has taken the form of referring people to local agencies.

The Kingdom of God is like two women who went to live on Bringhurst Street . . .

Covenant House has been described in such detail because

I see in it the marks of missionary action in the secular city. It can serve as a working model of what is meant by the secular presence of the church. It is a parable illustrating the spirit of the secular congregation. I realize that self-interpretation is risky but I am convinced that we are not going to be helped much today by theoretical blueprints of mission drawn up in some ecclesiastical executive suite. Rather, we shall learn what the nature of missionary action in our day actually *is* by observing specific, concrete, particular mission ventures.[2]

It should be understood that Covenant House came into being out of the life of our congregation. If there were no First Methodist Church of Germantown, there would be no Covenant House. But the House is not and never has been institutionally or organizationally related to the congregation. For two years it has had its own legal existence as an independent corporation. It is a private venture of a few of our people, joined by many others inside and outside the congregation. In recent years it has been blessed with the financial support and encouragement of the congregation. In turn it is helping to open the eyes and hearts of the congregation to our neighbors on Bringhurst Street.

There are two marks of mission in Covenant House that I believe to be integral to every authentic form of Christian mission in whatever locale: evangelism and covenant. In Chapters IV and V we shall consider *secular covenant*, the worldly holiness of Christians in their life together. In this chapter and the next we shall explore *secular evangelism*, the holy worldliness of Christians on mission in the world. We shall make this exploration by asking two questions. First, What is evangelism as embodied in Covenant House? Second (to be discussed in Chapter III), How can the local congregation become such an evangelistic community?

What Is Evangelism as Embodied in Covenant House?

"Evangelism" is a damaged term for many people today. It smacks of sawdust trails, crusade arenas, commitment cards, institutional hucksterism, and religious propaganda. It implies visitation campaigns and preaching rallies, and is almost entirely verbal in character. But I think "evangelism" is a term worth renovating because it makes clear (*euangelion*, Greek word in the New Testament) that proclaiming the good news involves *both the Word and the deed* of the Gospel. The deed without the Word is merely a matter of social service, important as it is, and the Word without the deed (and this is where the church has chiefly been guilty) is simply irrelevant piety, for which there is no longer any metropolitan audience.

George F. McLeod writes, "Since the content of our message has ceased to have any meaning (to most outsiders) we must begin at the other end by showing them community in actual operation. Something new must enter into their experience before they can understand the Christian message." McLeod is speaking of what I choose to call secular evangelism, evangelism whose shape, style, and language will be determined by the world, evangelism whose color will be strictly local, on-location evangelism, incarnational evangelism, with a priority not on sermonizing about the Good News, but demonstrating it, dramatizing it, embodying it, enacting it, sharing it. The three abiding principles of secular evangelism are: *discerning* Christ at work in the world, *participating* in Christ's work in the world, and *witnessing* to Christ.[3]

1. *Discerning Christ at Work in the World.* We are those who know that the risen Christ is alive in the world incognito. It is highly suggestive that in the resurrection stories Jesus appears first to his disciples as a stranger—the stranger on the beach, the stranger in the garden, the stranger in the Upper Room, the stranger on the road to Emmaus.[4] A stranger who gives us the clue as to where we shall meet him and sometimes recognize him today. "I was a stranger and you welcomed me . . . 'Lord, . . . when did we see thee a stranger and welcome thee' . . . 'As you did it to one of the least of my brethren, you did it to me' " (Matt. 25:35, 38, 40) Christ is the evangelist

hidden in our neighbor's need. His face is hidden in the faces of human need. He calls to us through our neighbor's need, as he called to Moses through the exploitation of the Hebrew slaves in Egypt, to the good Samaritan through the man half-dead on the Jericho road, and to Peter and John through the man lame from birth outside the temple in Jerusalem (Exod. 3:7-10; Luke 10:29-37; Acts 3:1-10). He goes before us to Galilee (Mark 16:7), to Jerusalem, to Emmaus, to Philadelphia, and to the city where you live, calling us to discern him in the human need present before our eyes. We do not find human need *only* in a poverty area, but also in "rich-young-ruler" suburbs, anywhere we will look for it and be open to it. Jennifer, Joan, and the Covenant Group discerned Christ at work in the human need of the Wister area in Germantown, and went to participate in his ministry there.

2. *Participating in Christ's Work in the World* means joining Christ in the specific human need that has been laid on you. It means the willingness to let go the nets of present securities and comforts to cross frontiers and go outside the walls in order to lodge with those one would serve. It means the willingness to let go cherished language in order to listen to the world and learn a new language. It means a world-oriented and located ministry, following Jesus, who, according to Mark's chronology, did not go into a synagogue again after being expelled from the one in his hometown, but carried on his work in the streets, public meeting places, and private homes. So Jennifer and Joan went to live on Bringhurst Street with all the risks involved, not to "go slumming" or to "do good" or to establish a beach-head for the institutional church, but to cast their lot with the people there— simply to live with them. Participating in Christ's work on Bringhurst Street includes a variety of health, welfare, educational, and community organizational ministries. But these ministries are all expressions of the basic fact of our *being*

there, as a House of hope in a neighborhood that had very little hope.

I recall sitting in the Covenant House living room with some forty House and neighborhood people watching a movie at our Christmas party. As I watched the children snuggling into the arms of their tutors, teachers, and friends; as I looked at the parents, whose friends we were becoming; as I saw the mural painting on the wall where the children had depicted their life on Bringhurst Street; as I felt the pressure on my arm of a boy whom I was then tutoring, I realized that the deepest thing happening on Bringhurst Street is not adequately described by health, welfare, community organization, education, or any other specific service, as valid and essential as they all are. The only term big enough is LOVE. If the purpose of the church is to "increase among men the love of God and the love of neighbor"[5] something of that increase is going on at Covenant House. And that is what it means to participate in Christ's work in the world.

3. *Witnessing to Christ.* This is the toughest one of the three principles of secular evangelism for us. As Bonhoeffer says, "What a difficult thing it often is to utter the name of Jesus Christ in the presence even of a brother."[6] How do we name Christ's name on Bringhurst Street? Should we name his name? There is a clue to the answer for our question in a remarkable program being carried on at the Massachusetts Correctional Institution at Norfolk, Massachusetts.[7] Some three hundred men go inside the prison several nights a week for conversation and fellowship with prisoners. When inmates are ready to be released, these "outmates" help them to get jobs, places to live, etc. One of the "outmates" writes, "Our emphasis is not on conversion in the old sense, but honest fellowship with men on the bottom of the social totem pole. For those "outmates" who become involved, the strangeness is that they begin to find the meaning of the New Testament in prison rather than on the outside, and with those whose

lives have been non-Christian rather than with the righteous ones." So the purpose of Covenant House is not conversion but community; not talking about Christ but seeking to welcome anybody and everybody to share His life with us.

We are being told that this is a time for silent witness; that the church has talked too much while doing too little; that God does not disappear if you fail to talk about him;[8] that we have lost the right to be heard; that nobody is listening anyway; that there should be a moratorium on talking for a generation while we listen to the world and quietly serve it. That makes sense to me. It suggests that among the images Jesus used for the church, "leaven" may be a most pertinent one for our time. It suggests that our style of verbal witness should be responsive and not aggressive—"Be ready at any time to give a quiet and reverent answer to any man who wants a reason for the hope that you have within you" (I Pet. 3:15, PHIL-LIPS). We are to wait until somebody asks what makes us tick, why we are there and what we are about. The trouble is, people seldom ask, for the simple reason that our lives are not so compelling as to bring forth such questions. But some times people do ask Jennifer, "Why?" Not long after Covenant House came into being, Jennifer was talking over our hopes with the man who was then president of the Wister Neighborhood Council. Toward the end of their conversation he remarked, "I don't know why you're here and I can't find the words to describe what you're doing, but either you must be a very good Christian or one of those young idealists. In any case you're a dedicated person." That man read Jennifer right. It was he who named the name of Christ. As Joan put it, "Since we had opened the doors to understanding, the truth had emerged naturally and easily. At such moments proclamation is woven into witness and the fruits of faith are filled with joy."[9] For Jennifer and occasionally for others of us on Bringhurst Street there are personal relationships and occasions when it is appropriate to share with another the reason for the hope that is within us.

But silent witness is not enough. "A church with silent witness is like a church without Easter." How does Easter become audible and visible in secular mission? If Easter is among us and in us, it will come out in ways and words that we cannot program or anticipate. Making Easter contemporary is the work of the Holy Spirit; and when the gift is given, people "catch" it because it is contagious. When Easter is real in our lives, words may not be necessary to communicate it. When Easter is not real in our lives, no amount of words can convey what is not there to be conveyed. A friend wrote in the early months of Covenant House, "What you're trying to say will take at least two years, and the measure of patience you exhibit while you wait will be the real test. I hope you can resist the seduction of mission as it is usually understood, and instead, truly become. When you finally learn more from your neighbors than you bring to them, you will be beginning to witness."

What are we learning from our neighbors?

We are learning about the extreme apathy of the neighborhood as exemplified by attendance of only three or four people at PTA meetings, and by the existence of more committees than people present at the Neighborhood Association meetings. We are learning that fifth-graders cannot tell time, second-graders do not know the days of the week, and all "graders" have only one opportunity, television, to reach any culture outside themselves. Effie, a nine-year-old boy who lives two houses down the street from Covenant House, when asked what he wanted for his birthday, replied, "A credit card and a gun!"

We are learning about the lack of communication between ethnic and racial groups on the street. The long-time white residents, primarily Italian descent, resent the intrusion of

Negroes, and the newer whites (polyglot) are hostile to both the Italians and the Negroes.

We are learning about the lack of communication in families, especially between husband and wife. The husband will go out with his friends, will take no responsibility for the raising of children; mothers have virtually no social life outside family groupings.

We are learning about self-respect. At a House party, one of my daughters gave a ball to a small boy, who handed it back and said, "I can buy one myself."

We have learned that a poverty mother with eight or ten children loves each of her children as much as an affluent mother with only two or three. We are learning about human generosity. After a Christmas party one year the children went caroling in the neighborhood. One woman was so moved that she gave a $10.00 bill to the group on her doorstep. After consultation as to what to do with it, the group marched to a house on the next block where it was known a family was in particular need, and presented the $10.00 to the mother of that house. Walking back, one of the children said, "I think Jesus was watching us tonight."

Our prefabricated images of poverty people are being broken. Jennifer reports that parents rarely bring their children to her medical office without cash in hand. The poor have learned by bitter experience to expect treatment only if they show their money first. At the same time, sick children are brought to her by older brothers or sisters when a mother is too tired or too drunk to bring the child herself. We are learning something of what it feels like to see all the good things of life literally across the street and be unable to reach and get some for oneself. At a circus one night, Effie wanted everything he saw—a hotdog, ice cream, soda pop, banners, clown's masks, hats, peanuts, popcorn, toy tigers, elephants, etc., etc. He was so frantic to touch and taste each new thing he saw, he could scarcely enjoy what he was presently touching or tasting. After years of the frustration of being unable to get the "good things" for yourself or your children, you can begin to understand how in a riot atmosphere you would take what you could get in a store broken open.

We are learning, as we fix up the House and our tax rates go up, how discouraging it is for an owner or landlord to spend money on a property only to be charged more for it in taxes as well.

At a party one night at which teenagers on the block put on a song-and-dance show for us (which was really swinging!), we learned how important it is for kids on Bringhurst Street to develop pride in their own talent and self-confidence—and how sad it is that there are so few opportunities for them to show what they can do.

We are learning how neighborhoods go downhill and start back uphill. The lot at the corner of the block was a shambles —broken bottles, cans, paper, refuse. A Neighborhood Committee was appointed to do something about it. Two years went by. Nothing happened. We wanted to bring in a work party of youth from outside the neighborhood to clean it up. But local social-work philosophy was, "Wait until the people themselves do it, or it won't last." So we waited, and waited, and waited. Finally one man on the block appealed to the Land Utilization Department of the city to beautify the corner, and it was done!

We are learning how hard it is for the poor to avail themselves of health and welfare facilities located at a great distance from them. A woman on the block who needed psychiatric counseling walked the three miles to the nearest such facility several times. Each time the venture took three or four hours in going, waiting to be served, and coming back. After a number of interviews which did not seem productive to her she stopped going, her problem unsolved. The effort was just too much for her. In an age of urban mobility, the poor are not mobile.

We are learning about the value of a neighborhood, and especially a poverty neighborhood. On the block there are several places of identification marking out the intangible, but felt, community known by residents. There is the school, the corner delicatessen, and across the street the laundromat; there is the bar around the corner, one's own house, Covenant House. We know that what needs to be done is not for an Urban Renewal program to wipe out all these signs of community and ship the present residents to "nowheresville" but, rather, to rehabilitate and beautify the present neighborhood. And we know it is the city's responsibility, working with local people, to do this job—in neighborhood after neighborhood across the city.

We are learning about the injustice of things. One evening in the middle of her prayers, our daughter, then aged seven, sat up in bed and said, "Daddy, it's unfair of God!"

"What's unfair?" I asked.

"God answers our prayers and we have everything nice; why doesn't he answer Effie's prayers and the other kids' prayers at Jennifer's house so they can have nice things too?"

I tried to defend God by pointing out that he expects us to share what we have with the children at Jennifer's House, and to improve the schools and get the fathers jobs so that they can get nice things themselves. But she knows that something's unfair about it, and someone's responsible.

There are Easter moments in the life of the House, moments when by the gift of the Spirit it is a truly open house and the new wine flows freely. The 1966 winter Newsletter describes one such occasion of secular communion, which no one planned. It just happened that way.

. . . the big room downstairs hugged its inhabitants in candlelight. A dozen children and half as many adults chattered amiably among the mounds of spaghetti at each place. Negro and white, young and old, shared together in a supper of need. Such was the occasion several weeks ago when one Bringhurst Street family of ten, which had not eaten a square meal in days, and several Covenant House families gathered for an informal banquet. It was, indeed, a Great Banquet[10]—unplanned, unanticipated, surprised by joy. This kind of gracious gift, couched in the guise of spaghetti and meatballs, continually calls us back from the clamor of event and accomplishment, to kneel before Him for whose Presence we give thanks.

Secular evangelism, as embodied in Covenant House, means to discern Christ at work in the world, to participate in his work and to witness to him. We now have a tool of analysis with which to examine the congregation and to ask the next question: How can the local congregation become an evangelistic community?

SECULAR EVANGELISM: The Congregation Without Walls

How Can the Local Congregation Become an Evangelistic Community?

INDEED, CAN it? I look with skepticism both on those who already know that God will not (cannot?) renew the present structures and on those who are blindly defending structures that died years or decades ago. It is clear that creative work can be done and is being done both inside and outside parochial structures, and that for a long time to come there will need to be both parochial and nonparochial structures, with increasing varieties of the latter. I believe that the most useful thing I can do is to share, from the inside of the parish I know best, what a congregation that is struggling to become an evangelistic community looks and feels like, in the hope that our experience will not be wholly alien to your own.

A bit of background. The membership of our congregation went from nearly two thousand in 1950, when the community was 12 per cent Negro, to fifteen hundred in 1961, by which time the community was 26 per cent Negro. By the end of 1967 our numbers had been reduced, hopefully in Gideon fashion, to eleven hundred and fifty persons. The loss reflects population shifts and the moving out or death of many of our people. Also, we have tried to make the membership roll more nearly conform to the actual number of those present and living. Some people, it should be mentioned, left because they were not in sympathy with one aspect or another of our program. We have been strengthened considerably by those who have come to share our life and work in recent years. In 1967, with the membership four-fifths the size of that in 1961, our pledging is approximately 25 per cent larger than it was then. Fewer people are giving more money. This is a small sign of the fact that in the congregation there may be no discernible relation between numbers and obedience, but the correlation between obedience and fruitfulness is real, if not always visible.

Our church has a beautiful memorial chapel whose doors to the street were closed out of fear of vandalism and the possibility of personal attack on people at prayer. After considerable debate among congregation officials, the chapel was opened on a twenty-four-hour-a-day basis. For several months a custodian was employed to be on guard between the hours of ten at night and four in the morning. (He estimated that about two hundred people a month were in the chapel between those hours.) Eventually an alarm system was installed.

The opening of the chapel doors was symbolic of what had to happen and still has to happen to our congregation. It was a small but significant way of saying to the community (and to ourselves), "We are no longer afraid; we want to serve you in this neighborhood; we want to know you and we want you to know us. Come in." It was symbolic of our turning inside out, from a primary concern to preserve our institutional existence to serving the people of the community. It was the opening of our little Vatican window, the beginning of our aggiornamento, the beginning of the secularization of our congregation, which has continued with much joy and cost to this day.

How Has Our Congregation Sought to Discern Christ at Work in the World?

Our idea of *mission* typically had to do with *missions*, usually foreign missions, far away from us and the farther the safer and better! For many years we had supported a missionary on the island of Vieques, Puerto Rico. About seven thousand Puerto Ricans live on the island some 1,800 miles from us. It shocked us to discover that less than eight miles from us in Germantown—in downtown Philadelphia—lived more than fifteen thousand Puerto Ricans. In terms of Jesus' charge to the disciples: ". . . and you shall be my witnesses [Where first?] in Jerusalem and in all Judea and Samaria and to the end of the earth" (Acts 1:8), we had as much, if not more, responsibility for human need at our back door, in Germantown and Philadelphia as in far-away Puerto Rico. Not that we should be unconcerned about the latter; but that we should acknowledge the prior claim of the former.

More importantly, we began to understand that there can be no integrity in our mission abroad if there is infidelity in our mission at home. This struck me forcibly some years ago when a layman of a large congregation in Jackson, Mississippi, bragged to me that his church held the record for the second-highest giving to foreign missions in the entire denomination. At the very time he was speaking to me, a Negro could not get in the back door of that church on a Sunday morning to worship God. (Happily that situation is now rectified.) But the point should be clear to all of us in our own situations: Obedience abroad can be a cover for disobedience at home. Obedience, like charity, should start at home, and reach to the end of the earth.

Any congregation in a metropolitan area, and especially suburban congregations, should regard the entire metropolis as its field of mission. It is unjust for Christians who derive their income from a city to deny responsibility for the welfare of that city by hiding behind suburban geography and politics. It is unjust for Christians to concern themselves only with the high-grade suburban schools where *their* children go, and not to be concerned with the schools of the city where most of the metropolitan area's children *have* to go. Christians and their congregations should find ways of bringing the resources of the suburbs to bear on the desperate needs of the city.

One suburban congregation doing just this is the Wayne Baptist Church in Wayne, Pennsylvania, near Philadelphia. Concerned about the slums of North Philadelphia, this congregation hired an expert to survey a particular area of North Philadelphia to ascertain housing needs and possibilities. Working carefully from this report and *together with local neighborhood citizens*, a housing corporation was created to buy, rehabilitate, and rent or sell housing. Suburb and slum are concretely joined together, to the mutual benefit of both.

Imaginative denominational and ecumenical leadership can point the way toward metropolitan government by acknowledging in their own programs and financial dispositions that the whole city is the mission field. A tragic negative illustration of this, in my opinion, is a decision made by a denomination in a metropolitan area some years ago. A decision was made to budget $650,000 for Church Extension (building new suburban church buildings) for the next several years, and for the same period of time $60,000 for work in the inner city of that metropolitan area. Ten times as much for suburban development as for the healing of city sickness! A modest amendment offered, to make the first figure $600,000 and the second $100,000, was voted down. One thinks of poverty and crime in our cities today and realizes that the church is guilty of neglecting the least of these jammed into urban ghettos, while spending and making money in the suburbs. Urban riots are a near-perfect contemporary illustration of Paul's words, "Do not be deceived; God is not mocked, for whatever a man [or a church or a city] sows, that he will also reap" (Gal. 6:7). We have sown cruel neglect of the poor and we are reaping riots.

Our congregation began to focus on our own neighborhood and its people. Our facilities, built for the use and benefit of our own members, and long since little used by them, could conceivably be of great benefit to the people of the neighborhood. When the late Robert Spike became the minister of the Judson Memorial Church in New York City, he had an architect survey their huge stone building to determine its possible uses. The architect reported, "Of one thing I can assure: your church is militarily defensible." So is ours! To many in our community our building was a forbidding fortress dotted with closed and locked doors. The first thing we had to do was to take our walls down, to unlock and open our doors quite literally to all sorts and conditions of people and groups in the community. So in recent years neighborhood gangs, SNCC, the Angry Arts (a group of Philadelphia artists protesting the war in Vietnam), and the Get Set Program have used our buildings along with the usual community clubs and organizations. Our Board of Trustees deserves much credit for its open-door policy of the use of church buildings by responsible groups.

The second thing was to find out what Christ was doing in the community: i.e., who are the least of these and where are they (and who are the most of these and where are they); who is alienated from whom in the community (where is there controversy); what walls of hostility need to be broken down (Matt. 25:31 ff.; 2 Cor. 5:16-20; Eph. 2:11-18). Where there is unmet human need, there is Jesus Christ. The church is to provide "help to the helpless"[1]—to try to meet human needs currently not being served in the community until such time as secular agencies recognize the need and begin to meet it, allowing the church to withdraw and move on to some other need not being acknowledged or served.

We asked a number of neighborhood leaders to tell us what some of the unmet needs in Germantown were. They ticked off a list of items typical of any urban area suffering population shifts, commercial deterioration, and physical decay—a tutoring program for the hundreds of youth dropping out of the high school across the street, wholesome recreation for youth after school hours and in the evenings and on the weekends, job employment and vocational training for youth, recreation and imaginative care for the large elderly population, etc.

Any congregation that takes a "Matthew 25" survey of its immediate neighborhood and metropolitan community, and listens to the people who live there and not just to community "leaders" or agency people, will find out what Christ is doing there. State hospitals, prisons, Public Housing projects, nursing homes, homes for the aged and for children groan with desperate human needs. Several years ago the Church of the Saviour in Washington, D.C. "saw" Christ at work in Childrens' Village, an institution for many orphaned and/or unwanted children in that city. The members of the congregation devoted themselves to *emptying* that institution, creating a mission group FLOC (For Love of Children). So far they have worked together with other congregations and persons to reduce by more then one hundred the number of children there.[2] Indians, migrant workers and other un-enfranchised or disfranchised groups cry out for help. If a congregation has eyes to see, it will see. It will discern Christ at work serving the human need in its community and go to participate in his work.

How Has Our Congregation Sought to Participate in Christ's Work in Germantown and Philadelphia?

We may speak of Christ's work in biblical language as bringing good news to the poor, release to the captives and deliverance of the oppressed, and bringing peace, and unity and reconciliation, and serving the least of these, or loving the neighbor (Luke 4:16-21; Eph. 2:14-17; 1:10; 2 Cor. 5:18-20; Matt. 25:31 ff.; Mark 12:28-31; Luke 10:25-37). We may speak of Christ's work in contemporary language as making a city or a nation or a world more truly and fully human, as healing the urban fractures, as acknowledging the solidarity of mankind and working toward a single new humanity in the world (Eph. 2:15, NEB). And we may speak of the particular ways in which a given congregation may appropriately seek to do these things in its own place. The following concerns (some are shared by all the congregation; others involve just a few) are intended to portray the what and how of our congregation's participation in Christ's work. It is not suggested that any other congregation should follow our pattern. On the contrary, we believe that each congregation literally has to work out its own salvation (faithful participation) in response to Christ's work in its own unique circumstances. But particular patterns and experience may be suggestive both as to what to do and what not to do.

A. Youth. Our ministry to youth includes: tutoring, recreation, employment, the Glass Door, and gangs. For four years now we have had a tutoring program involving at any given time about fifteen tutors and sixty or more young people. The improvement of some youth was so impressive to school authorities that a foundation grant was secured for two years to enable professional tutoring in addition to the volunteer program. While the value of tutoring is manifest, its limitations include, more often than not, a lack of continuity in the tutorial-student relationship and inability to get at the root of the cultural problem whose symptom is expressed in the need for tutorial help. Tutoring is just a beginning.

Out of involvement with the youth in this way we began to see their need for recreation. For several years we have opened the building for basketball, dances, art classes, refreshments, etc.—and provided program leadership. Before long we saw the great need for employment. One summer my colleague Ted Loder persuaded some community leaders to fund a program to hire thirty to forty young people to do rehabilitative work in the area. Two years later our colleague Jerry Rardin established an employment service in an attempt to find jobs in the community for teenagers. This was one of the factors in the emergence of a substantial and continuing youth employment service operated by the Germantown Community Council.

The Glass Door came into being in the winter of 1965, the brainchild of Jerry Rardin, funded by a special offering from the congregation, and dedicated to provide not only the specific services of tutoring, recreation, help in finding employment, but also a place and a chance for youth just *to be*. The Glass Door is a place to talk, to listen, to dance, to be together. It is a kind of teenage hangout, open several nights a week during the summer and at least one night a week throughout the year. Typically it is open from 8:30 P.M. to 11:30 P.M. It is a large room with a "glass door" opening onto an alley behind the church building—hence its name. It has been remodeled, with a rheostat to dim the lights in theatrical style, a snack bar complete with stove, refrigerator, etc., and a changing collage of signs, art work, bulletin boards, and miscellaneous paraphernalia. One sign reads: ALL ADULTS MUST BE ACCOMPANIED BY A RESPONSIBLE TEEN-AGER. One night there will be a combo brought in to play for a dance; another night a Black Muslim, or a police officer, or one of the young people will speak; another night just games and talk and something to eat and drink. Sometimes gangs have moved in, discipline has not been adequate, and we have had to call the police. Racial composition has varied from a fair mixture of Negro and white to predominantly Negro.

In the spring of 1966 a local Negro who is a probation officer was hired by the church on a part-time basis to work

with gangs—of which there are at least four discernible in
Germantown at the present writing. Several months later a
second man was employed in the gang ministry. In the summer of 1967 several congregations joined in the gang ministry
to make it ecumenical in organization and funding. Currently, therefore, the Glass Door has a dual focus: an
ecumenical gang ministry largely carried on in the streets with
occasional uses of the Glass Door facility, and a program of
dialogue and dancing for the general youth "public." Several
hundred local youths have been involved in the Glass Door in
recent years. Some casework, especially assisting youth in the
police station or in court, is done; and employment continues
to be a concern. Now led by John Rice, it is a valuable
tool for working with youth in Germantown. Our experience
in the youth ministry indicates that one simply grabs onto
the spoke of the wheel of youth-need that is nearest at hand,
and as he moves in closer to the hub, the other spokes begin
to appear. The important matter for a congregation is to grab
a particular spoke and get going.

B. Race. Our congregation has slowly been integrating. At
first it was a source of frustration to me that such a small
percentage of our membership was Negro (currently about 3
per cent, with 10 per cent of every new membership class
usually Negro). Factors include the presence, two blocks
away, of a strong and prominent Negro Methodist church,
the wide number and variety of integrated congregations in
Germantown, the relative formality of our liturgy, and the
effects of the Black Power movement. Today I am content
with wherever the membership chips happen to fall. If a congregation is honestly wide-open to everyone in the community
and honestly involved in seeking to serve the people of the
community, the percentage of racial mixture is a secondary
matter. We are not called to have a specific percentage of
Negroes in the congregation; we are called to serve and love
and welcome into our fellowship *all* the people of the com-

munity. Action for racial justice has involved some of our people in picketing and demonstrating, and many more in writing letters to local and national officials concerning the issues of open housing, civil rights legislation, the Girard College Case in Philadelphia, etc. In the winter of 1967 four congregations (two Episcopal and one Jewish suburban congregation and ours), participated in what was called a Black Power/White Power course. The course had first been given at the Wayne, Pennsylvania, Baptist Church and was organized for us by the Wellsprings Ecumenical Center (see p. 53). Each congregation provided at least fifteen people for the six-session course which met in each of the congregation's buildings at least once. Black Power advocates of the Philadelphia metropolitan area "confronted" these people with the black man's feelings toward whites, his frustration, bitterness, anger, and determination to organize the Negro community for its own political and economic purposes. It was an explosive experience for many white liberals to discover that Negroes are not sitting around feeling grateful for white good will that changes nothing. Awareness of the need for direct social action and community organization to effect social change does not come easily to most white liberals. A direct result of the course was the forming of concrete relationships between some people in Chestnut Hill (a wealthy suburb) and North Philadelphia (a ghetto). A storefront office was opened in North Philadelphia as a focal point for bringing together the needs, the resources, and the people of the two areas. The venture was called "Operation Pipeline." The Black Power/White Power course was given in three other regions of the metropolitan area and was the model on which the courses in the fall 1967 Germantown *Ecumenical Institute* were based. This Institute, co-sponsored by Wellsprings and the Religious Council of Germantown, involved more than 400 persons of Germantown-area churches and synagogues in ten courses which were held over a six-week period.

Course titles were: Grass-Roots Political Action, Renewal of
Religious Institutions, Jewish-Christian Relations, Roman
Catholic-Protestant Relations, Black-White Relations, Issues
of War and Peace, Women in Society, Lay Theology, Moral
Crises of Technology, Youth-Adult Film Dialogue Seminar. A
clergy seminar was also held.

C. *War and Peace.* There is no more divisive issue in America today than the Vietnam war. How is a congregation to
relate the gospel to the most burning dilemma of the nation?
How is a congregation to be helped to hold the Bible in one
hand and the daily newspaper in the other and to see Vietnam
in the light of the gospel? This much is clear:

1. Nobody has a hot-line from God—least of all the
preacher.

2. Everybody—especially the laymen—has a right to be
heard.

3. There is no official "God-position" or congregational
position.

4. The pulpit must be absolutely free for whoever preaches.

Many sermons on Vietnam have been delivered to our
congregation—the prevailing temper being that of responsible
dissent from government policy. Congregational classes and
debates on Vietnam have kept the congregation aware of the
issues. Some concerned people have participated in peace
marches, in prayer fasts, and many more have written letters
to congressmen and signed petitions. My guess is that there
are at least as many hawks as doves among us. There is an
appropriate form of action for everyone, and it is the task of
the clergy to persuade or goad everyone to do what he feels
called to do. The one thing we cannot do is do nothing, give
up, lose hope that our letters and actions and prayers are of
any avail. That option is not open to the Christian. As Paul
reminds us, ". . . be steadfast, immovable, always abounding
in the work of the Lord, knowing that in the Lord your labor
is not in vain" (1 Cor. 15:58). It is at least possible that the

Church could make a major assist in mobilizing national senti-
ment (as in the passage of the 1964 Civil Rights Bill) to
change administration policy from escalation to negotiation.

D. Ecumenism. In 1962 Pope John opened the Vatican
window. In 1967 it seems beyond question that neither Pope
nor Council will be able to close the Vatican window. With
the crumbling of an ancient authority, which is rocking the
Roman Catholic Church today, one can understand Pope
Paul's concern to hold the church steady. But one remembers
Peter's reply to the disapproving religious authorities of his
day: "We must obey God rather than men" (Acts 5:29). The
Holy Spirit finally will have his way. In the meantime the
breeze is fresh, the winds are exhilarating, bishops beware,
and Christians of the world breathe deeply! While top-level
ecumenism is of great importance, its successes and failures
may ultimately prove to be chiefly reflections of the grass-
roots ecumenical dialogue and action taking place across the
country and throughout the world. One example of this is the
Wellsprings Ecumenical Center in Philadelphia. Wellsprings
is an interracial, interfaith group of laymen and clergy devoted to the renewal of metropolitan Philadelphia, and to the
renewal of their own congregations and themselves. Started in
July 1964 as a dialogue group of people from many congregations and meeting in the homes of participants, Wellsprings
moved through several months of personal conversation and
the developing of trust and friendship to the point of action. A
Roman Catholic layman was employed as Director of Wellsprings in the fall of 1965, and in November of that year the
Ecumenical Center was established in a storefront on Germantown Avenue. (The personal gifts of Wellsprings' members and friends made the venture possible.) Ecumenical con-
ferences, seminars, retreats, services of common prayer, etc.,
were held. An ecumenical library began to develop at the
Center, appropriate magazines and periodicals were put on
display, a news-clipping file was established. There was a

place of identification, a headquarters. Jewish participation
became a reality in 1966; significant denominational and
foundation support came in 1967. In September of that year
a Jewish woman became Associate Director of Wellsprings
and a Negro woman the center co-ordinator making the
dream of an interfaith inter-racial staff a reality. A major
ecumenical institute co-sponsored by the Religious Council
of Germantown was held in the fall of 1967 and the program
of "exporting" courses such as the Black Power/White Power
course throughout the metropolitan area, was expanded.

The value of Wellsprings, apart from its immeasurable personal meanings, is that it does not suffer (yet) the stultifica-
tion of so many "official" religious agencies and councils of
churches. It is free to work with and for such authorities, but
independently of them and always in direct contact with "the
people" responding to events and trends quickly and competently. It is able to do some things that neither individual
congregations nor denominations nor councils of churches
seem able to do. It seeks to replace none of them, but rather
to strengthen people in their own religious tradition, and to
serve in this time of institutional breakdown as a flexible and
mobile signpost of the Spirit at work in the world and in the
church. Its reach always exceeds its grasp, and there is as
much change as continuity. But every community could use a
Wellsprings, and it takes only two people (of different faiths)
to start one.

E. Work. A concerned businessman asks, "How do we
change the outlook of a whole society so that we as a nation,
business as companies, and people as individuals get on the
side of the 'have-nots'? How does change within an institution
take place; who has to be reached, how can they be reached?
How can business' action be implemented on behalf of the
'have-nots' without undermining the whole structure of the
private enterprise system which, in my view, is clearly the
most efficient system of doing business that man has come up

with so far? How can I be an effective agent of such change within my own corporation?"

Who can help the man with such questions? His clergyman? No! To expect a clergyman to help him would be like expecting a citizen of one country to be able to explain to the citizen of another country, whose language he does not speak and whose ethos he does not breathe, how to live, move, and have his being in that other country. We clergymen, for the most part, do not *know* the world in which our laymen work. The man who asked those questions can be helped only by fellow workers who share his context and his questions, and perhaps by specially trained laymen and clergy who become knowledgeable about that particular "work world" and competent to serve as resource and research persons. Metropolitan Associates (MAP) was established in Philadelphia with the support of several denominations in 1965 to research what it means to be a man and a Christian in the complex "worlds" of the modern metropolis. The man who asked the questions above participated in the Business and Industry Sector Group of MAP in 1966-67. He explored with other men the myth systems by which any and every corporation (including the one for which he works) live, and began to understand his role as an agent of social change within that corporation as his *Christian* vocation.

MAP, a nonparochial research organization, is helping men to discover their occupational *vocation*, and these men in turn are helping others in their own secular structures search out their occupational vocation. Every city could use a MAP, and all it takes to get one going is brains, imaginative ecclesiastical support, and lots of good men and good money.

F. Art, Drama, Music, Dance, etc. Artists are "the spiritual alarm clocks," the secular prophets of our day. (The church used to be the patron of the arts, but now most artists are alienated from the institutional church. A jazz pianist recently commented to a minister, "I believe but I don't belong.")

How can the church reach out to the artist, seeking to learn from him rather than to "tell him"? How can the church affirm the artist and his art as valuable in its own terms, apart from "religious" meanings we may find in it?

One way to get at all of this is through an arts festival. Many congregations are having such festivals these years. Our congregation has had three, the most recent lasting an entire week in the spring of 1967. What has happened to us in these festivals?

We have learned that art is an incomparably more exciting and enriching vehicle of praising God than we had imagined. We have watched the chancel of our sanctuary, our "holy of holies," secularized by plays being performed in it on a Saturday night, a jazz quartet playing in it on a Sunday afternoon, and a woman dancing in it during a worship service on Sunday morning (as well as civil rights rallies and other public meetings). Psalm 150 has "come alive" among us:

> Praise the Lord!
> Praise God in his sanctuary;
> . . . .
> Praise him with trumpet sound;
>   praise him with lute and harp!
> Praise him with timbrel and dance;
>   praise him with strings and pipe!
> Praise him with sounding cymbals;
>   praise him with loud clashing cymbals!
>   Psalm 150:1, 3-5

Praising the Lord must have been an exciting and noisy celebration in those days! Why not now? How we pallid Protestants have restricted the music and art that are "acceptable" vehicles of worshiping God on a Sunday morning. How joyless our worship often is.[3] Our junior high class taught us this vividly when they put on, with the help of Jerry Rardin, their own Pentecost service a month after the Arts Festival in May, 1967. Their processional hymn was "When the Saints Go

Marchin' In." Many of them preached and prayed, definitely "in their own language." At the offertory an original dance was performed by three young people in the chancel. The dance was their interpretation of the folk song "Lord of the Dance,"[4] and was accompanied by guitar and the singing of the song by the other participants. The recessional hymn was the rhythmic song "Amen."

Is God less pleased by guitar than organ? Does he prefer to be praised by Bach more than by the "Blues"? Does he like "For All the Saints" better than "When the Saints Go Marchin' In"? Our Youth are teaching us that Jesus as the "Lord of the Dance" is much more compelling to them (and to many of us as well) than Jesus as the lamb of God. They are teaching us that we are to be our real, worldly, honest selves in the chancel and not some phony "Gothic" self.

Sue Rardin, one of four laymen who reflected on the Festival in Sunday morning worship on the Festival's last day, said:

". . . perhaps we could trust . . . that the creation is so good that while the mind can teach the body, the body too—eyes, ears, fingers, muscles—can strangely perceive and act out true and good things that then can teach the mind its understanding. Perhaps our own human talents are not only a way of speaking but a way of listening. It is only through a kind of body-wisdom that a tiny baby learns he is loved by his parents. Concepts and words are no good to him. But we can use words and concepts. For us, especially those of us who aren't really artists, aren't words and concepts enough for us to learn by? Or do we still need that nonrational body-wisdom to know and tell each other that in this world we, and all men, are loved. All this week some familiar Scripture has been running through my head with an unusual *literal* implication: 'The eye cannot say to the hand, "I have no need of you," nor again the head to the feet, "I have no need of you" ' [1 Cor. 12:21]. Certainly they cannot, if it is true that feet and eyes and hands have their own miraculous ways of learning the good news behind the creation. After this week, I can almost wonder whether even the rhythm in a tapping toe is not trying to tell us something important."

We have learned something about the body-wisdom of God in the Incarnation by respecting and rejoicing in our own body-wisdom. We have begun to see and appreciate the religious dimension of all art without having to put religious labels on it. We have found friendship with artists, and our own creativity has been stimulated. Each festival has found more of our own people sharing their artistic gifts of drama, painting, dancing, singing, cooking, weaving, sculpture, music, etc. A drama group and "Listening to the World" groups (see p. 91) came out of the second festival. Annual film festivals and plays and monthly gallery displays in our social hall keep us sensitive to the artist and his art and to our own throughout the year. A Youth Arts Program in the church school, pioneered by Louise Curry, is of growing significance.

And not least of all, we ourselves are changed. Ted Loder, who, together with Louise Curry and the Fine Arts Committee was chiefly responsible for the organization of our recent Festival, put it this way on the last day of the Festival, "We have walked with giants this week." As we walked we grew more than a little "to mature manhood, to the measure of the stature of the fullness of Christ" (Eph. 4:13).

Youth, race, war and peace, ecumenism, work, art—these are some of the human concerns our congregation has discerned in its "Matthew 25" survey of our community. Other concerns currently being explored include mental health, housing, and ministry to the aged. Doubtless the reader can identify these and many other such concerns in the mission field of his own congregation. Discernment leads to participation, and participation to witness.

How Has Our Congregation Sought to Witness to Christ?

Participation in Christ's work *is* witness to him. Jennifer and Joan first touched the edge of our congregation's life via a civil rights rally, not a preaching crusade or a visitation campaign. They came within range of our congregation because we were involved in a human issue of concern to them. Most of the people who have joined us in recent years have come primarily because of our involvement in the vital human issues of Germantown, Philadelphia, and the nation (and for a worship service in which sermon, singing, and praying celebrate such involvement).

All these modes of participation are in the deepest sense of the word "evangelistic." They cannot hope to solve the problems of the city but, rather, they are signposts of the kingdom of God in our midst, parables of God's love in action, just as Jesus' deeds of healing were signs. When the disciples of John the Baptist came to Jesus asking if he were the Messiah, Jesus replied, "Go and tell John what you have seen and heard; the blind receive their sight, the lame walk, the lepers are cleansed, and the deaf hear, the dead are raised up, the poor have good news preached to them" (Luke 7:22). Jesus pointed to the things that were happening, and invited John's disciples to decide what their significance was and who he was.

So we are to take down our walls, coping with the "blessed messiness" of it all[5] as we engage in the healing and humanizing work of secular evangelism.

As we do so, inquirers and unbelievers will begin to participate in one aspect or another of our life and work. As they have studied with us, served with us, and sometimes worshiped with us, we have realized their tremendous importance to us. They probe our presuppositions, open up our narrow theologies, and enrich our understanding of what it is to be human (and thus, what it means to be a Christian). They keep us more honest than we would be without them.

One Sunday I preached a pastoral sermon on "forgiveness," of which many of us in the congregation were, at that time, in great need. That week a letter came to me from one of our non-Christian friends who happened to be worshiping with us that Sunday. In it she criticized the sermon I had preached. "You made it much too easy for all of us. Instead of encouraging us to get out and demonstrate to end the war in Vietnam, to get out and try to clean up the slums in the United States, you offered us God's forgiveness for our lack of action. I am sure that if the historical Jesus were alive today, he would be leading us on marches, in work camps, and down the road to free men from all types of prisons. Please, don't let us leave church comfortable. We need encouragement to go out and love people in the ways that are not easy."

It is our humiliation as Christians that often we, who bear the name of Christ, are less faithful witnesses to what he stood for than some of those who do not bear his name. Bearing the name is no guarantee that we are bearing the Cross. We remember that Jesus said, "Not everyone who says to me 'Lord, Lord' shall enter the Kingdom of heaven, but he who does the will of my father . . ." (Matt. 7:21). Some of those who do not bear his name on their lips, do bear his Cross in their lives. They are the hidden, the latent church, the people with whom we are finding a friendship deeper than that of mere creedal affirmations.

An avowed atheist, who is Executive Director of a private Urban Renewal Corporation in our community, joined forces with our congregation when he saw that we shared his concern for the human renewal of Germantown. He was deeply moved by Jennifer and Joan's moving onto Bringhurst Street. It was he who wrote our Lay Leader during the pledge crisis of 1964 urging that our congregational program not be cut back and giving tangible support to that end. When the three ministers of our congregation, together with three laymen, participated in the Selma-to-Montgomery March in 1965, he came with us.

I discovered something very important in those two days together with him. I realized that I felt closer to him as a human being than to some people who acknowledged the name of Christ. I realized that God is at work in him, though unacknowledged by him, and that I could be grateful for him as a friend and partner in the struggle to heal a wounded world without having to put Christian labels on any of it, and without worrying about his eternal salvation or mine. As H. Richard Niebuhr put it, "We Christians are not those who are being saved out of a perishing world, but those who know the world is being saved."[6]

Does it matter whether he believes in the God of Jesus Christ? Would it make any difference to him? I don't know. He says of his own faith, "Life is a practical matter here on earth where it begins and ends. We must do the best we can. We will miss out on something important if we don't cherish the friends, love, beauty, etc., of the passing scene. While I am a kind of fatalist or determinist, the basic difference between us may be that I neither judge nor wish to do so, any ultimate nature of reality. It's simply here; I work with what I can perceive of it, and let the tail go with the hide!"

Perhaps the basic difference between us is "hope." My friend believes that history is empty of meaning or purpose and that Death is our destiny. He has no ultimate hope.

Because I love that man I hope that some day the good news that there is hope may become real for him, and that he may know whatever men know when they come to believe that history is *full* of meaning and purpose signifying everything, and that Life is our destiny. For we are those who have been given hope. Ultimate reality has disclosed itself to us in Abraham and Moses, and pre-eminently in Jesus, as our Father. This news is good! It gives us hope for this world and the world to come.

SECULAR COVENANT: The Covenant Group

"Covenant" is a crucial biblical word. It describes God's relation to his people and theirs to him and to each other. God calls us into covenant for the purpose of "saving" the world (i.e., "reconciling the world," "uniting all things in heaven and on earth," "healing the nations," etc.; (2 Cor. 5:19; Eph. 1:10; Rev. 22:2). The Old Covenant was born in the Exodus deliverance. "And Moses went up to God, and the Lord called him out of the mountain, saying, 'Thus you shall say to the house of Jacob, and tell the people of Israel: You have seen what I did to the Egyptians, and how I bore you on eagles' wings and brought you to myself. Now therefore, if you will obey my voice and keep my covenant you shall be my own possession among all peoples; for all the earth is mine, and you shall be to me a kingdom of priests and a holy nation'" (Exod. 19:3-6a).

The context of the Old Covenant was secular. The covenant was born out of what God did through the defeat of the Egyptians, God's action in secular history (under Pharaoh) for the purpose of creating a people to be a light to the nations (Isa. 49:6). The content of the Old Covenant was embodied in law, the Ten Commandments written on tablets of stone. The Old Covenant was celebrated by a sacred meal to commemorate the Exodus deliverance (Exod. 12:1-14).

The New Covenant was born in the Easter deliverance. "By his great mercy we have been born anew to a living hope through the resurrection of Jesus Christ from the dead. . . .

you are a chosen race, a royal priesthood, a holy nation, God's own people, that you may declare the wonderful deeds of him who called you out of darkness into his marvelous light. Once you were no people but now you are God's people; once you had not received mercy but now you have received mercy" (1 Pet. 1:3; 2:9-10).

The context of the New Covenant was secular. The covenant was born out of what God did through the life and death of Jesus, God's action in secular history (under Pontius Pilate), for the purpose of re-creating a people to be a light to the nations. The content of the New Covenant was embodied in a new commandment to love God and neighbor (Mark 12:28-31), a commandment written on human hearts (Jer. 31:31-33). The New Covenant was celebrated by a sacred meal to commemorate the Easter deliverance (1 Cor. 11:23-26).

Throughout the history of the old and the new Israel, people have been bound together by covenantal agreements. Sometimes the covenants have been specific—as is the case with the Puritans, the Wesleyans, the monastic orders where membership vows are explicit and demanding. Sometimes the covenants have been general—as is the case with the Roman Catholics, the Anglicans, and "main-line" Protestant churches where membership vows are implicit and undemanding. At all times and in all places the church is God's covenant people bound to him and to mankind in the responsibilities of love for the purpose of saving the world. It is God who saves. It is the church which is called to be the covenant people. The content of the covenant is provided by the church. The context of the covenant is provided by the world. Covenants, therefore, are temporary and flexible, changing with the changing shape of secular events.

With this biblical background, we are now ready to explore the meaning of "covenant" in the emerging secular congregation. In Chapters II and III we considered "secular evan-

gelism," the *mission* of the church in the world. In this chapter and the next we shall consider "secular covenant," the life
together of Christians. The Covenant House Group will serve
as a parable of what is meant by covenant in the secular
context. As we see how a small group, focused on a specific
and limited mission, works out its own covenant in response
to its calling and circumstances, we shall better be able to see
how the large congregation might go about shaping its own
covenant, appropriate to its calling and circumstances. We
shall explore the meaning of "covenant" by asking two questions: First, What is "covenant" as embodied in the Covenant
House Group (the subject of this chapter)? Second, How can
the local congregation become a *covenant* community (the
subject of Chapter V)?

What Is "Covenant" as Embodied in the Covenant House Group?

Covenant House was born out of the Covenant Group.
You will remember that ten people found themselves drawn
together by a common concern to serve human need in the
Wister area of lower Germantown. We believe that we were
truly "called together." No one got an idea and then sold it to
others. There was the strong conviction of the Holy Spirit's
power in the emergence of this small community. It was not
so much that we consciously caused things to jell, but that
things seemed to fall into place. There was a common sense of
the fullness of time, and the wonder of each person serving his
unique role in the shaping of the mission and of our life together. Joan described the early life of the covenant community:

For our little gathering those first few months were very special.
Seeds were sown; fruits were realized, shared and re-sown. It was
that glorious time when faith bursts forth into so many crystals it
seems that not even the heavens are able to contain their bounty
and beauty. Meeting once a week, in Bible study, prayer and

discussion, we came to know and love one another: two ministers, a businessman, a newspaper reporter, the wives of the four, Jennifer and I. We bound ourselves in *covenant* to pray everyday for each other, for the Church out of which our mission has grown, for ecumenical involvement in all that we were doing, for the city in which we were living.[1]

The context of the covenant was secular. It was born out of what God was doing in lower Germantown. The content of the covenant by which we lived from March, 1964, until June, 1965, was explicit and demanding.

We are seeking to be God's instruments in His world. In our search we make this covenant. It binds us each to the other in the name of Christ. We do this because we believe that one way we can see more clearly God's purpose for us, and Christ's power in us, is through our unconditional commitment to love one another. We do this because we seek together to hear God's Word for today's world and to act on that Word. We do this because we believe that a Christian discipline needs to be specific. Thus we mutually agree to:
    —pray for each other every day
    —study selected passages from the Bible every day
    —meet together once a week for study and worship, sharing our lives together
    —seek the direction of a Christian mission in Germantown
    —make a monthly financial contribution to the mission
    —give whatever is required of our time and talents and resources to the mission
    —participate in and be sustained by the life of our local congregation
    —be open to every possibility of ecumenicity in the mission
    —sanctify these mutual commitments by sharing together in the sacrament of the Lord's Supper.

"Work and worship were closely woven into our life together. From painting walls and scrubbing floors, we would move toward prayer together; from our Bible study we would move out into the local political structures or the laundromat.

In spite of the difficulties of a limitless pile of details, too much physical work for the time available, and lengthy meetings, we felt drawn by something beyond ourselves."[2] Looking back we can realize that those first few special months were the honeymoon period of the mission. We can rejoice in that time while recognizing that a honeymoon is but a prologue to making a marriage or a mission work. Frustrations accompanied our decision to wait an entire year before undertaking specific services or programs in order to give Jennifer and Joan time to establish a natural neighbor presence. Needs appeared all around us, and we were impatient to respond to them. Tensions arose within the Group. Some of us felt that we were spending proportionately too much time on study and discussion and too little on-location in the work of the House. The covenant, which had harnessed our mutual commitment to bring the House into being and had enabled our nourishing in those intensive months of mutual discovery, now seemed burdensome.

So in June, 1965, we suspended the covenant. We gambled on the hope that we could continue the work of the mission without meeting together for study and prayer. At first, there was an audible sign of relief as we enjoyed our freedom from the discipline of the covenant. But within a matter of weeks, some of us began to be uneasy. A feeling began to grow that we were without a sense of direction, that there was an emptiness at the heart of the House. Along with the loss of mission-direction came the loss of personal commitment. Since we were no longer meeting regularly, confidence that we were still praying for each other waned. Because one's own commitment was fading, one inevitably wondered about the commitment of others. The erosion of the fellowship and the drifting of the mission were under way.

Experiencing this erosion and drift taught us our need to be "housed" again, in a covenant more appropriate to our changing circumstances. So in the fall of 1965 we regrouped; two members of the original group dropping out and four new persons joining us. It was agreed that the new covenant should focus less on reflective discussion and more on the work of the mission. We decided to meet together only twice a month instead of every week. The new covenant centered on the verbs *work, give, pray, meet*. It eliminated the requirement of *daily* prayer and Bible study. We wanted the covenant to be concrete without being a strait-jacket, specific and yet with flexibility, so as to underline the essential aspects of our life and work while encouraging diverse modes of participation according to our individual temperaments and circumstances. It was agreed that the new covenant should have limited tenure, and that after a year it would be subject to reappraisal. So we began the year of 1966.

That summer found the Covenant Group embroiled in two important questions. The first was a problem of organization. The whole program of the House mission was devolving upon Jennifer by virtue of her being on location (Joan having left for seminary). The burden on her had become intolerable and the rest of us had been unable to take enough of the responsibility off her shoulders. It became clear, finally, that either some other person would have to take the role of coordinating the variety of House activities or Jennifer would have to move out of the House. This occasioned the second question.

Was the House only a place of *doing* (a place where certain services were offered) or was it also and essentially a place of *being* (a place where someone lived.) Was it basically a settlement house or a home? If it was essentially a place where a variety of services was offered, then the residence of Jennifer was not indispensable. But if the residential aspect of the House was integral to the purpose of the mission (if we were to *be* there for others) then Jennifer or someone else must *live* there, not simply work there on a nine-to-five basis. We had discovered by then that a settlement house operating on a nine-to-five basis may be regarded by many local people as something of an alien presence. A settlement house has, of course, its own legitimate work to do, and there may be little to distinguish between such an agency and Covenant House in terms of visible programs. But the fact of Jennifer's residence makes the House honestly a home, and enables those of us who cluster around Jennifer helping in the mission to be something of a family. And it enables some of us (the Covenant Group) to be a celebrating core in the heart of the House.

We reaffirmed our basic and original conviction that the essential witness of the House is a witness of *being*, out of which the varieties of doing (services and activities) emerge as branches from a vine. We also reaffirmed our conviction that the essential witness of the House is corporate, built on the residence of a least one person, but including all (local people and workers from outside the neighborhood) who participate in the life and work of the House. Our purpose was not only to provide specific services but to help create community on the street. We wanted the House to be an "open" House.

Immediate steps were taken to employ a person part-time to coordinate the activities of the House. This was done with funds generously provided by First Methodist Church. (One-half the Easter Offering for Urban Mission was given by the church to Covenant House in 1966 and 1967.) It will be recalled that Covenant House was not then and is not now organizationally related to the church or under its administration. This gift in 1966 marked the first major financial support of the House from the congregation, and was matched (for two years) by funds from the Board of the National Division of Missions of the Methodist Church. The coordinator greatly relieved the burden on Jennifer. By the fall of 1967, as House activities expanded, the coordinator role had grown to a half-time job.

Another important event late in 1966 was the formation of Covenant House, Inc. This action allowed tax deductible gifts from individuals, institutions, and foundations to be made to the House. Six members of the Group, and one other person important to the House mission, were designated as directors of the Board of Covenant House, Jennifer being made the president of the Corporation. The first Annual Meeting of the Corporation was held at the House on January 13, 1967. The Board was given responsibility for carrying on the *business* of the mission. The Group was to be the context for both reflection about the lives of members and reflection about the mission. The Board, therefore, was an objective, administrative body; the Group a subjective, leading body. The Board's purpose was to carry out with integrity the leading of the Group; the Group's purpose was to listen to, and try to interpret with integrity, the leading of the Spirit based on study of the biblical word and the life together of prayer and mutual responsibility.

We can examine the covenant of the Group more closely, exploring its threefold rubric. The covenant gives specific shape to the kerygma, the koinonia, and the diakonia, or as we shall translate those terms, the Word, the priesthood, and the mission. How were we exposed to the Word and involved in the priesthood for the sake of the mission?

1. *The Word.* Central to the covenant was the hearing and appropriation of the biblical gospel. The Bible was the written vehicle par excellence of God's living Word to us as persons and as a mission group. Our Bible study was not so much academic as pragmatic, in the sense of exposing ourselves and our work to the judgment and direction of God. This confrontation with the biblical Word was accomplished in the beginning by weekly study of an agreed-upon passage. Many would read the passage daily, pondering the meanings of words and verses, jotting down insights and questions, allowing new meanings to emerge from one day to the next. A passage that

was impervious at first or second reading might yield a fresh insight at third reading. Events in our own lives or in the neighborhood or the nation plowed the ground of our awareness so that a verse of little relevance early in the week might take deep rootage later in the week. When we came together we shared the fruits of our individual study. Sometimes the discussion was routine; most of the time the richness of insights gathered provoked new thinking and fed us deeply.

It was the most productive Bible study in which I have been personally involved. I think there are three reasons for this. First, we were deeply committed to one another and to the mission. All of us had a good deal at stake personally. This personal dimension—call it faith—opened us to the Spirit and to each other in our study. Second, we read the biblical passages *daily* and met *weekly*. So there was an intensity and immediacy about the biblical word as we wrestled for its meanings. Third, the focus of the study was specific and concrete. We would ask ourselves, "What is God saying to us as persons and as a group about the work of the House, our own lives, and our friends on the street?" We were middlemen, with our ears listening for the Word, and our eyes on the world of Bringhurst Street. We used commentaries but would not allow ourselves to be confined by them. We discovered the potential power of the bare words themselves (not in a fundamentalist sense) not yet explicated, tied up and perhaps corraled by a commentary. It is important to know the historical and linguistic facts concerning a particular passage. But at the same time no commentator can possibly anticipate ahead of time how God would speak his Word to us in our particular context through this particular written word.

We began our study in March 1964 with Paul's Letter to the Ephesians, wondering what God would do with us, what the mission would be to which he would call us. It seemed that Paul was praying not only for the Ephesians but for us when he asked that God would reveal his purposes, "having the eyes of your hearts enlightened, that you may know what is the hope to which he has called you" (Eph. 1:18). That hope took shape much sooner than we had expected. For in May of that year, only two months after the Covenant Group had formed and our study had begun, we found ourselves buying a house, a house of hope in a neighborhood that had very little hope.

That first summer we began to study the Gospel according to John. In the fifth chapter we came upon the episode of the healing of the man who had been ill for thirty-eight years (John 5:2-9). We saw the people on Bringhurst Street, suffering from chronic poverty, to be not unlike that multitude of invalids waiting for help around the pool. Here on this street were people sick with the virus of poverty, failure, and hopelessness for longer than thirty-eight years. The crucial question for them, and for us as individuals, was, "Do you want to be healed?" It may be easier to stay sick than to go through the pain of getting well. It happened that my thirty-eighth birthday occurred the week we studied this passage. There were lesions in my own life at the time, and I quickly identified with the man who had been ill for thirty-eight years. I heard that question addressed to me in the first-person singular, "Do you want to be healed?" I can remember praying for several days afterward, "Lord, I want to want to be healed."

As we studied the tenth chapter of John, it was Jennifer who reminded us that "they do not know the voice of strangers" (John 10:5). It would take some time and living before Jennifer's strange (British) voice and all of our middle-class accents would become familiar. We were reinforced in our decision to wait a year before undertaking specific programs, a year during which the stranger might become a friend whose voice would be known and welcomed on the street.

In the thirteenth chapter of John we were struck by the fact that the new commandment was to "love one another"; "even as I have loved you; that you also love one another. By this all men will know that you are my disciples, if you have love for one another" (John 13:34-35). If we were not able to love each other, how could we presume to love our neighbors, much less our enemies? We have needed reminding again and again that the authenticity of our love for one another is the heart of whatever witness we hope to make on Bringhurst Street. Whatever we may do or say, what we are in terms of our relationships together and our concern for our neighbors for their own sakes constitutes the deepest reality of the mission.

As we wrestled with the complexities of living and working together in the covenant, the study of the letter to the Hebrews spoke to our condition. We were impressed with the humanity of Jesus who "had to be made like his brethren in every respect . . . [who] is able to help those who are tempted . . . because he himself has suffered and been tempted" (Heb. 2:17-18). We were discovering some of the selfishness in ourselves, previously unsuspected but now brought to the surface by the pressure of week-by-week exposure to one another. Somehow we were grateful that Jesus knew every kind of pressure and temptation that we were knowing. He seemed closer to us and more real because of his sharing our humanity. And therefore we could turn to him for help. "For we have not a high priest who is unable to sympathize with our weaknesses, but one who in every respect has been tempted as we are, yet without sinning. Let us then with confidence draw near to the throne of grace, that we may receive mercy and find grace to help in time of need" (Heb. 4:15-16).

A recurring question in our meetings was whether or not we should make verbal witness on Bringhurst Street, and if we should, how we should do it. In our study of Acts we noted "the boldness" of Peter and John, who forcefully defended themselves before public and religious authorities, and stated that they would have to obey God rather than man (Acts

4:13-20). How were we to be bold on Bringhurst Street? We agreed that we should be ready to speak up clearly whenever, in a personal conversation, it seemed appropriate. (Though Jennifer did mention the near impossibility of talking about Jesus Christ in the course of examining a case of diaper rash!) But we felt that Christians today are called to be bold primarily in action. So, when the junkyard dealer across the street from the House sought legal endorsement for expanded operations, Jennifer and another woman on the street got sixty-five signatures on a petition seeking to block the endorsement. Several signers received anonymous threatening phone calls warning them not to sign. Our cause lost on a legal technicality. But it did teach us the necessity of working through City Hall and the courts to effect basic changes on the street, and it was certainly the first experience in participatory democracy for many of those who signed the petition.

In the tenth chapter of Acts (esp. vv. 34, 44-48), we were intrigued by Peter's astonishment in discovering that God was working through Cornelius, a Gentile. Peter was amazed to find out that the Holy Spirit does not always work through "channels" (i.e. the covenant people) but through outsiders as well. The Holy Spirit had broken the barrier between insider (Jew) and outsider (Gentile) which Peter had believed to be ordained. His thinking about how and through whom God works was radically secularized in the recognition that "God shows no partiality" but works through all men. Peter's discovery was pertinent to what we were discovering. For it was plain that the Spirit was working in and through outsiders (non-Covenant Group members) in the work of the House, in powerful ways. In fact, Cornelius after Cornelius showed up, in the form of a woman on the next block who became one of our two nursery school teachers, a young gynecologist who started the Family Planning Clinic, a South African woman who became our coordinator, the man on the block who got City Hall to fix up the corner lot, a woman in the

neighborhood taking leadership in organizing parents in the
school PTA, neighborhood youths who organized their own
tutoring program, and dozens of other people. It was not that
they came to us, but that we became aware of them and what
they were already doing or were willing to do. In fact, the
Word of God seemed often to come to us more decisively
through such new persons and events in the neighborhood
and at the House than through our Bible study. One summer
evening in July, 1967, there was a House party in the backyard. The planned entertainment fell through, and instead, a
group of teenagers on the block put on a song-and-dance
show for us. And they were great! The girls singing and sway-
ing and snapping their fingers; the boys on the drums; the
record player turned high and something to eat and drink
afterward—a secular communion in which the Lord was
surely with us, as he was with those men in the Emmaus
restaurant (Luke 24).

So our neat categories crumbled, as Peter's had, and we
found ourselves blinking the eyes of our hearts at the ways
and means of the Spirit. If we are less clear in our doctrine of
the Holy Spirit we are more clear on the validity of unexpected "happenings" whereby the Word comes to us through
Cornelius persons and events.

2. *The Priesthood.* We were totally unprepared for the exuberant joy of those early months together. The mutual discovery of the mission and of each other as new friends took us
by surprise. It was sheer gift, like finding a pearl of great price
or a treasure in a field (Matt. 13:44-45). One of us wrote at
the time: ". . . there came the dawning realization that it
wasn't just that we respected and loved all of you, but that we
were loved . . . the tremendous, glorious joy of sharing laughter, and ideas, and prayer together. I think the very angels
must be rejoicing in our joy, and I begin to comprehend
Paul's outbursts of exultation in the working out of God's
purposes. I am sanely and soberly (as much as is possible in

these intoxicating days) convinced that together we will discover and, in fact, are now learning something of what the
kingdom of God is like."

There is always joy when a child or a friendship or a mission is born. I think the reason much of the joyous language
of the New Testament sounds exaggerated to us is that we do
not often have such experience of God's gift of life and love as
to justify such language. We sing the hymn "O for a Thousand Tongues to Sing," but one tongue is plenty for most of us
most of the time. Or perhaps we are embarrassed as well as
surprised by joy. I believe that joy, doxology, is an abiding, if
not consistently experienced, dimension of Christian life. And
I am wary of new mission ventures which do not have such a
time of joyous wonder at the pentecostal power of the new
thing God is doing. In authentic Christian mission, as exemplified throughout the book of Acts and Paul's letters, joy in the
morning is normative.

But noon comes very soon. And if God gives us a special
joy in the birth of our priesthood, perhaps it is to help us
through the inevitable time of disillusionment with each other
and ourselves. As we moved into the second year of living in
the covenant, the pressures of time and energy on all of us
forced us to revise "our unconditional commitment to love
one another" as it was stated in our first covenant. We found
that we could not love each other unconditionally; we could
not even love the members of our families without conditions.
In fact, we are told to love only God with all our heart, mind,
soul, and strength. So our unrealistic expectations of one another and ourselves were broken, as we all sought more
soberly to understand our commitment to each other and to
the House as a part of our multiple commitments to spouse,
parent, child, colleague, other friends, congregation, community, etc.

Being accountable so relentlessly week-after-week forced
us to become aware of weaknesses in our nature which had

successfully remained hidden before. We began to see into the ambiguity of our motives and those of our brothers and sometimes reached the limits of our capacity to understand, accept and forgive, or accept forgiveness. The "lowliness and meekness with patience, forbearing one another in love" (Eph. 4:2) which we read about, was not easy to grasp. We found ourselves judging and being judged. It was hard to have to learn that the strong and the weak need each other, and harder to learn that "each of us is *both* weak and strong."[3] Through it all our egos were being pruned and our real selves began to emerge. We began to understand, as we had not before, our need to pray for each other; to pray for love we did not have or even want at times. We learned that praying for one another is not an optional luxury for a Christian community, but a desperate necessity. We grew to understand Bonhoeffer's observation:

It is the freedom of the other person that is a burden to the Christian. The freedom of the other person includes all that we mean by a person's nature, individuality, endowment; it includes his weaknesses, and oddities which are such a trial to our patience; everything that produces frictions, conflicts and collisions among us. To bear the burden of the other person means involvement with the created reality of the other as he is, to accept and affirm it and in bearing with it, to break through to the point where we are able to take joy in it.[4]

The joy is given to us, not always, but again and again like the deep affirmation of a Bach fugue. We know one another better than we know most others, and we are known by these friends better than by most others. We have been reconciled many times and there is confidence in the power of God to keep enabling us to grow in mutual understanding and encouragement. A verse from our study of Colossians aptly expresses what we have learned to hope and pray for each other and our friends on Bringhurst Street. "May He strengthen you with ample power to meet whatever comes with endurance, patience, and joy" (Col. 1:11, NEB).

On April 8, 1967, we met in one of our homes to celebrate three years of life and work together at the House. Several friends of the House joined Group members as we gathered around an elongated family table, heard the story of the two men who had supper with a stranger in that Emmaus restaurant, and then shared bread and wine and a delicious dinner. There was clever poetry and gifts for Jennifer, whose birthday had occurred two days before. There was a devastingly funny parody on each member of the Group enacted by one of our number, and farewells to the Rardins who were shortly to leave Philadelphia. We concluded with a discussion of the Resurrection and what meanings we found in that Emmaus incident. We are beginning to understand why the sharing of food and drink was such a significant aspect of Jesus' ministry (Mark 2:15-17; 6:34-44; Matt. 11:19; Luke 7:36-50; 11:37-41; 19:1-6; John 2:1-11), why he liked to speak of the kingdom of God as a great banquet (Mark 14:22-25; Matt. 9:14-17; 22:1-14; 25:1-13; Luke 14:1-24; 15:20-24; 13:22-30) and why our ordinary meals now and then become extraordinary celebrations (Luke 24; John 21).

The fall of 1967 was a time of major rethinking for the Covenant Group. Jennifer made an exciting and startling proposal to us in the form of a letter. She noted that for the first two years of the House mission, the Group had provided the essential guidance and strength. In the third year, however, the Board increasingly became the decision-making center of the House as the mission expanded, the financial details mounted (foundations as well as congregations and over fifty persons were now supporting the House work), and the task of coordinating activities assumed major proportions. As we reflected on how people on the block might be invited to share in the decisions about the work of the House, we could see that the Board was a more natural, less pious and threatening, context than the Group. The Board was already more ecumenical in composition than the Group. So the question was raised before us: was the Board the new wineskin appropriate to receive and release the new wine pouring into the House from so many unexpected directions? In the fullness of time was the Board a secular structure now more suitable as a vehicle of the Spirit's work than the Group?

The question was not easy to answer. We can never be sure when it is time to change a structure or to seek renewal of persons within a structure. The truth was that the Group had become stultified, the Bible study not as productive as before, the meetings less vital and creative. Was God closing one door and opening another? Letty Russell gave us perspective from the experience of the East Harlem Protestant Parish. She wrote:

Everything about these functional types of structures of witnessing communities is fluid except that they are "witnessing communities," communities gathered together by Christ, that they might be equipped to join in God's mission of restoring men to their true humanity. (a) They are fluid because the membership of the groups is always changing. People are free to belong to one or more groups at the same time, and to move from one group to another. (b) They are fluid in that they do not all possess, all the time, all the basic characteristics of a witnessing community. A group may not have sacramental celebration with Christ, or it may not have common Bible study and reflection. Members of the group may feel that this is not possible because of the presence of so many non-Christians who are sharing in the common serving function.[5]

Jennifer's proposal was that the Group members should disperse into one or the other of the missions of the House—tutoring, the Family Planning Clinic, nursery school, library, medical practice, counseling service, etc. In fact each Group member already was in one of these missions. But the new idea was that each of these missions (in which several local and non-Group people were involved) might have its times of corporate reflection. This was already happening in the nursery school mission, where a mothers' group had been meeting for over two years, and in the tutoring mission as well. The proposed corporate reflection might take whatever form was appropriate in each case. Representatives from each mission would be elected to the Board, and thus the Board would become a truly ecumenical, secular, and increasingly indigenous context of reflection on the work of the House. There would continue to be House parties, "issue" meetings, and occasionally Bible study and sacramental celebration for those who wanted to participate in it. The covenant would now be written in our hearts (Jer. 31:31-33) and our working, praying, giving, and meeting would take place chiefly in dispersal.

At this writing, Jennifer's proposal is being discussed. It is painful to think of giving up a structure which has been so personally rewarding and so fruitful for the work of the House. After only three years we are reluctant to let go familiar customs and are even defensive about them. But it is promising to think of moving into a structure which holds so much hope for creative mission at the House in the future. Is this perhaps a parable of the way God constantly calls his covenant people to move on and out, not knowing where or what or when or how, but trusting him to reveal in ever new ways the hope to which he has called us?

Albert Camus speaks for us when he says:

Let us not look for the door and the way out anywhere but in the wall against which we are living. . . . Great ideas . . . come into the world as gently as doves. Perhaps, then, if we live attentively, we shall hear, amid the uproar of empires and nations, a faint flutter of wings, the gentle stirring of life and hope. Some will say that this hope lies in a Nation; others, in a man. I believe, rather, that it is awakened, revived, nourished by millions of solitary individuals whose deeds and works every day negate frontiers and the crudest implications of history. . . . Each and every man, on the foundation of his own sufferings and joys, builds for all.[6]

SECULAR COVENANT: The Congregation with Roots

How CAN the local congregation become a covenant community?

The changing secular context makes old covenantal forms inadequate and calls for new forms appropriate to the new conditions. For example, in 1900 in Independence, Iowa, where my father grew up, the Sunday morning worship service of the Methodist Church was an adequate celebration of the covenant of that congregation. The people who gathered in that congregation for worship knew each other, for better and for worse, intimately. Every day of the week they worked, talked, fought, played, loved, and hated together— learning to live a corporate life of permanent stability. They were literally stuck with each other. Their interdependence in that small town was visible and acknowledged. They belonged to each other, like it or not. So when they worshiped, they came as an authentic family to be judged and pardoned. The biblical word fell on ground that had been plowed all week. A child was baptized into a genuine congregational family of people who could honestly commit themselves to aid the parents in teaching and caring for the child. The Lord's Supper could embody the corporate brokenness of those who came, and the whole congregation could thus be judged, healed, and restored to human community again. It did not, of course, always happen that way. But the structure was an adequate vehicle for celebrating God's presence in the life and work of the people, and the membership vows expressed a congregational covenant that was in its own terms real and honest. There may still be many towns and even closely knit neighborhoods in cities and suburbs where the Sunday morning worship service continues to be an adequate structure to celebrate the life and work of the covenant community.

But in 1967 in metropolitan Philadelphia the Sunday morning service of the urban or suburban congregation is no longer an adequate vehicle *by itself*, to celebrate the life and work of the congregation. People gather for worship in unconnected anonymity, often not knowing even the names or recognizing the faces of those sitting on either side of them in the pew. They may come from many parts of the metropolitan area. The only life they share together all week is the one hour of Sunday morning worship. They are not stuck with each other, but live lives of constant mobility. Their independence of each other and lack of mutual belonging is virtually guaranteed by the anonymity and mobility of the metropolis. So when they worship, they come together as isolated individuals or families who typically conceive of their relation to the congregation in voluntaristic and private terms. They come not as a family but as a lonely crowd. The biblical word falls on ground that has not been corporately plowed. The sermon is given the impossible burden of trying to re-create a covenant community which is not even in existence. The lack of authentic community in the congregation makes it like an audience and the minister like a speaker or entertainer. The Lord's Supper, instead of being a family celebration, is reduced to a hope for individual inspiration. Baptism, instead of being the congregation's joyous acknowledgment of a new member in the family, is reduced to a sentimental or socially proper ceremony.[1]

In such a congregation there is inauthenticity or disintegrity of membership, and the membership vows strain to express a covenant life which in fact is nonexistent. In such a congregation there is an emptiness, a deadness, a lack of depth in the experience of Sunday morning worship.

The Sunday morning worship service is no longer an adequate structure by itself for celebrating the life and work of the metropolitan congregation. The changing secular context requires new forms apart from public worship where people can be welcomed into the covenant community and equipped for secular evangelism in the metropolis. We must redefine the focus of entrance into the congregation as entrance into the covenant community. We must redefine the focus of exit from the congregation as exit into the world as missionary persons and groups. The church today needs new "calling" and "sending" foci. When these new structures are born, discovered, and put into operation, the weekly congregational service of worship on Sunday morning, or some other time, will once again be able to celebrate the power and the glory of God's work in our midst.

I suggest three actions which can be taken to enable the congregation to become a covenant community.

The First Action Is to Reshape the "Come" and "Go" Structures of the Congregation

The "come" structure is that by which we welcome people into the life of the congregation. The "go" structures are those by which we involve people in serving the world.

A. *The "come" structure is whatever we require or do not require of seekers and of ourselves at the point of membership in the congregation.* It is the visible way of saying who we are, whose we are, and what we are about. The lack of significant membership preparation for adults in most Protestant congregations after more than fifteen years of the "renewal" movement in the church, testifies to the fact that newcomers are not coming into a covenant community which either we or they regard as significant. Conversely, in congregations where rebirth of mission is taking place, preparation of new people for significant participation in the life and work of the congregation is regarded as both a primary opportunity and a responsibility. (The one exception to this, with which I am familiar, is the Judson Memorial Church in New York City [see p. 135, note 17] where newcomers are grafted almost on sight into the work of the congregation, and where membership, if it comes at all, comes after many months of genuine involvement in the congregation's life. The congregation itself, about one hundred in number, is the training context. Currently those at Judson are contemplating giving up the whole "membership" idea.) At the Church of the Saviour in Washington, D.C., two years of study and participating in the life of the congregation are required before membership is granted.

Somewhere between two years of preparation and the one right hand of fellowship on a Sunday morning offered by most congregations is a style of membership training which is appropriate for every church. Whatever its form and duration, its purpose will be to introduce people to the covenant community: to expose them to the Word by study of the Bible and other books, lecture, and discussion; to set them in the context of the *priesthood* by relating them to members of the congregation who will study, talk with, listen to, pray for, and worship with them during the time of preparation; to invite them to identify themselves potentially, if not immediately, at some specific place of service in the mission of the congregation.

There are two stages in the present membership orientation program of our congregation in Germantown. The first stage, named the "Christian Faith and Life Seminar" and consisting of six consecutive weekly meetings, is mandatory. We speak of "orientation" for significant participation in our life and work so that it is clear that every newcomer, even if he has been a Christian for fifty years, needs to come in order to discover what the inside of this particular congregation is like and how he may best fit into its life and work. Since I have described the nature of these six meetings in detail elsewhere,[2] a brief analysis here will be sufficient. The lay leaders gather at 7:00 P.M. on Sunday for final discussion of the theme of the evening, exchange information about the people in the seminar, and pray for the power and sensitivity of the Spirit to be released among us in the seminar. At 8:00 P.M. the people come to the church parlor (two of the six meetings are held in the homes of the co-ministers). The order of events is:

8:00 *Opening witness by a layman.* This usually includes a brief Scripture reading, a personal expression of what this particular person is struggling with in his faith or life—what he has found, what he is looking for—concluding with prayer.

8:15 *The theme of the evening presented.* This is done through a talk by one of the ministers, a panel of laymen, a skit or drama by laymen, a reading, dialogue, etc. Themes change; at present our six themes are, in order of presentation:
　　1. The Mission of the Church (one of the ministers)
　　2. God　　　　　　　　　　　　(one of the ministers)
　　3. The Good News of Freedom and Forgiveness (skit by laymen)
　　4. Prayer (panel of laymen)
　　5. Service in Congregation and Community (panel of laymen)
　　6. Worship and Celebration of Lord's Supper (one of the ministers)

9:00 *Small-Group Discussion.* These groups of about ten people are led by laymen; the ministers are not present. People are encouraged to express their questions, disagreements, discoveries, i.e. *themselves,* as they are and where they are. In these group discussions the Word is responded to, the priesthood is experienced, and the varieties of service are explored.

9:45 *Conversation and Coffee.* Often very important personal conversations take place after the seminar is officially over.

> People are open, friendships are established, ministries of
> listening occur, and the covenant community begins to be
> born for, and with, the new people and present members
> as well.

The seminar is for all new people some sort of new beginning.
We can help them to take it seriously and hopefully, as a time
when the Spirit may waken us to new insights, discoveries,
friendships, commitments. We urge each person to read at
least one of the many books in our church library or bookstore, and write a written report as a vehicle for expressing
who and where he is in his own pilgrimage of faith. We con-
clude the final meeting with a simple celebration of the Lord's
Supper, sitting in the church parlor where we have been meeting. Facing one another round a circle, the bread broken and
passed, a single cup passed by the people themselves, one to
the other (the priesthood of all believers), a spirit of joy as
well as penitence—the Lord's Supper becomes a real and
deep celebration of the covenant community which God has
given to us in the course of the seminar. For many newcomers,
it is the first time Communion has "broken through" with
power and meaning.

The second stage of the present membership-orientation
program is participation in a koinonia group,[3] formed of
members of the seminar and lasting a year. This is optional.
While we believe that a year in such a group provides the
most adequate structured way into the heart of the congregation's life, we have found over the years that koinonia groups
are not for everyone and that for some people another vehicle
such as a "Listening to the World" group (see p. 91) or
adult class on Sunday morning is to be preferred. However, for
many newcomers, a koinonia group provides opportunity to
engage in serious Bible study, to be part of a group of people
acknowledging in ways of service and prayer mutual responsibility for each other, and to find out who they are and where
they may best serve in the mission of this particular congrega-

tion. While some such groups may continue indefinitely, experience indicates that most will be wise to terminate after a year or so unless some corporate mission emerges which can serve as the focus of their continuing covenant. The greatest value of a koinonia group, in my judgment, is that it provides a context for new insights, friendship, healing, empowering. But soon the focus of our life together should be the specific ministries to which we are individually and corporately called, what are termed here the "go" structures of the congregation.

B. *The "go" structures are the various ways and groups whereby we equip people for secular evangelism in the metropolis.* We are not speaking here of the various established commissions and committees of the congregation which are necessary to its ongoing institutional life, and of which we will speak in a moment. Rather, the "go" structures are those task-oriented mission groups emerging from the life of the congregation or outside of it into which our people are called. Such structures are found in specific services, in the doing of which the Word is to be heard and the priesthood known. Let me illustrate the variety of ways in which some "go" structures have emerged in our congregational experience.

1. The Glass Door (see p. 49) came into being out of the consideration of the Education, Evangelism, and Christian Social Concerns commissions of the congregation. It was authorized by the Official Board and given financing by the Finance Commission. In the spring of 1967, other churches began to share financially in the gang ministry of the Glass Door. It is hoped that the ecumenical participation will grow, and that perhaps eventually the gang work may be supervised and funded by a separate ecumenical board.

2. *Wellsprings* (see p. 53) came into being as a few people from our congregation and several other congregations committed themselves personally and financially to it. It is incorporated and has an interfaith and interracial board.

Many congregations and four denominations are now giving it financial support.

3. The Mental Health Mission Group arose out of a koinonia group. A few of the original koinonia group dropped out and other people concerned about mental health joined. The group took volunteer training at the Norristown State Hospital. They began, in informal ways, to relate to people going into and coming out of mental hospitals. They have become a kind of therapy group seeking to work with other people in Germantown concerned about mental health, for more adequate counseling and therapy services in the community.

4. The MAP Business and Industry Sector Group came into being as a result of the work of Metropolitan Associates. One of our laymen became involved in the sector group studying the renewal of corporations such as the one for which he works.

5. Covenant House (see p. 22ff) came into being out of the life of the congregation but is not institutionally or organizationally related to it. The congregation has provided a climate of such freedom and creativity that new forms of mission such as the House have arisen out of its life, some of which are not under the congregation's administration.

Letty Russell describes such mission groups as either task-force communities, which come into being only for the purpose of doing a certain job and then stop or are changed in orientation when the job is finished, or "structures of permanent availability," which provide certain permanent services to society.[4] The signposts of these new "go" structures are fivefold. Not all the signs need be present in any particular mission but all are potentially there in every such mission. The structure will be *secular* in time and place; *ecumenical* in composition; chiefly composed of *laymen*; shaped around a *specific human need* or *issue*; and it will *work*. As Paul Chapman writes, "The real strength of any revolution is not a criticism of the old structures, but the effectiveness of the new structures."[5] As the "come" and "go" structures begin to do their work of receiving people into the covenant community and sending them into the world as missionary persons and task forces, the "old" structures of the congregation—the commissions, committees, and other organizations—the "stay" structures, are reinvigorated.

The Second Action Which Must Be Taken to Enable the Congregation to Become a Covenant Community Is to Reinvigorate the "Stay" Structures

Every institution lives through "stay" structures. The question is not whether the congregation will have "stay" structures, but whether these structures can receive and release throughout the whole congregation the new life engendered by the "come" and "go" structures. Only through the "stay" structures of committees on Education, Membership, Finance, Fine Arts, Mission, Worship, etc., can the whole congregation be redirected and empowered for the mission of secular evangelism in the world. The Faith and Life Seminar can bring people into the membership who are eager to participate in such a mission. The experimental ministries can open the eyes of the congregation to poverty, unemployed youth, gangs, inadequate schools, housing, mental health care, etc. But it remains for the Finance Commission of a given congregation to allocate the resources of the congregation to support such a missionary program. It remains for the Education Commission to learn how to educate the adults and young people of the congregation for such mission. It remains for the Fine Arts Committee to enable us to see and listen to the world we seek to love and serve, through films, drama, painting, dance, etc. It remains for the Missions Commission to educate and expose us to the major social, political, and economic issues of the day and to teach us that every such issue is a theological issue and every question about the neighbor is a question about God. It remains for the Worship Commission to discover what kind of liturgy excites and expedites the celebration of such a congregation's life and work. It remains for the Official Board or Session of such a congregation to commit its personnel, program, and resources to engage in the mission of a secular congregation. It will take years for the insight and power of the new ministries to invigorate and permeate the entire congregation. It will take years for the whole congregation to be turned inside out. And when it happens, it will happen through the "stay" structures, which will themselves be reshaped and reinvigorated in the process. And it will happen through many of the "stay" people, who themselves will have been turned inside out over these years.

Whether this congregational transformation happens is a matter of grace, luck, and hard work. Sometimes the circumstances of a congregation are such that it cannot happen without a rending split requiring painful years of healing. Sometimes a congregation has the good luck of sufficient resources and time to withstand severe shocks in its corporate life without going to pieces. Congregational transformation is not something that can be engineered. Whenever it begins to happen in even the smallest ways, it is a gift, it is a wonder, and it is a privileged joy in which to participate. Finally, the people themselves, in growing numbers, must want such transformation or it will not be possible. This means that the clergy and lay leadership of a congregation must pursue a strategy of wooing, winning, and waiting, while seeking to engage more and more of their people in secular evangelism. However, there are observations to be made about how the "stay" structures are reinvigorated. Specifically, we can ask: How is the whole congregation brought under the Word and involved in the congregational priesthood, while engaged in the mission?

The Word

A. We advocate the use of a congregational lectionary. The purpose of a lectionary is to involve the entire congregation (it is hoped) in reading the biblical passage which is to be the basis of the sermon the following Sunday. An exegesis or study guide in *Tidings*, our congregation's weekly newsletter, enables people to read more knowledgeably. Sometimes a commentary is available in the church bookstore for those who wish to study more deeply. Often koinonia groups will study the lectionary passages, using commentaries in addition to the actual sermons preached as source material. One fall, as we preached through Genesis, one of the koinonia groups studied Gensis and *The Secular City* in tandem. A lectionary provides a structured discipline for the preacher and in addition serves to "defend the Word against the preacher," as P. T. Forsyth once observed. The more the congregation knows about a given passage the less successful the preacher will be in riding his own hobbyhorse through that passage or distorting it to suit his own homiletical, psychological, or theological needs and ends.

Our general lectionary plan for a year is more haphazard than coherent. One year, for example, we preached through Philippians from September to Advent; spent Advent with Isaiah; explored Exodus from Christmas to Lent; lived with the Gospel according to John during Lent; and considered the doctrine of the church via Ephesians from Easter to Pentecost. Then we took the summer off for free-wheeling preaching.

We believe it makes sense for a given congregation to work out its own lectionary. Borrowing a lectionary fashioned in another context and for another congregation, or in a denominational office for no congregation in particular, robs us of the responsibility of shaping our exposure to the biblical word in ways appropriate to the particularities and peculiarities of our own congregational life and work. Liturgy is the expression of who we are and what we are called to do in a particular place and time. Therefore, we need to create our own fresh liturgy as faithfully as we seek to create fresh forms of life and mission. How the Holy Spirit works through our haphazard spirits in shaping our lectionary is known only to Him.

B. *Study Groups.* We have offered koinonia groups as the primary context for Bible study in the congregation. Groups vary considerably in their modes of study. Some groups use commentaries; some study nonbiblical books in commentary on biblical themes. An effective introduction to Bible study has consisted of placing passages in novels or plays in dialogue with biblical passages, the Word and the world in conversation. One group acted out a number of the parables, as background study using Thieleke's book *The Waiting Father.*[6] The result was considerably heightened meaning by virtue of the actual participation in the drama of the parable, hilarity in the selection of the "cast," and the shock of self-recognition that occasionally surprised a "player" as he saw *himself* in his role.

"Listening to the World" groups were developed by Ted Loder several years ago, and have provided a fresh and creative way of listening to God speaking to us through contemporary artists, dramatists, and novelists. Authors whose works have been read and discussed in recent years include John Updike, Nicholas Katzanzakis, Saul Bellow, Edward Albee, J. D. Salinger, John Osborne, Ignazio Silone, Archibald MacLeish (his *J.B.* was read concurrently with the biblical book of Job), Ernest Hemingway, T. S. Eliot, Truman Capote, Graham Greene, etc. Sometimes films or plays are seen and then discussed. This approach allows "the world" to ask its questions in its own language, and enables us to recognize ourselves in these questions. People who are uncomfortable in the more "pious" context of a koinonia group, or who do not profess Christian faith may find a "Listening to the World" group an open-ended way to explore new ideas. I believe that this approach to common study is a most significant contribution to the modern church as it seeks to enable people to enter into the dialogue between world and gospel.

In the Fall of 1965 a seminar was held on "The Meaning of Suffering." Meeting in the homes of participants (as is the custom with almost all our study groups), the group studied Aeschylus, *Oedipus Rex*, Job, Shakespeare's *King Lear*, Dostoevski's *The Brothers Karamzov*, Faulkner's *Absolam, Absolam*, and Bonhoeffer's *Letters and Papers from Prison*. The purpose of the seminar was to explore the suffering portrayed in these works, stretching and deepening our own understanding of suffering. The following year a seminar on "The Meaning of Death" was held. Tolstoy's *The Death of Ivan Ilyich*, Camus's *The Plague*, James Agee's *A Death in the Family*, and selected poetry by John Donne, Emily Dickenson, and T. S. Eliot provided various experiences and viewpoints of death for our consideration, and the opportunity of sharing our own experience with the death of relatives and friends.

Last year an experiment was conducted with teachers for the junior high and high school departments of the church school. Teachers were paid a token sum, and were required to participate in a teachers' seminar that met twice a month through the year, as well as to participate in retreats, parties, and other activities with their students. The seminar was taught by a professional theologian in our midst, and consisted of an intensive study of H. Richard Neibuhr's *The Responsible Self*. Many participants felt it was the most fruitful study in which they had ever engaged in the congregation. It is hoped that this seminar may be extended to more teachers in the years ahead.

C. *Adult Classes on Sunday Morning.* For many years our congregation has offered a women's and a men's Bible class, taught by highly competent persons among us. A few years ago an additional adult class was started to serve increasing numbers of our people who could come in for worship and study on Sunday morning but could not as easily participate in a class or study group on a week night. Professional theologians were invited to teach, and appropriate texts were assigned. A Lutheran gave eight lectures one year on Bonhoeffér's *Ethics* and Roman Catholic priests gave lectures on the Second Vatican Council. A rabbi lectured to us on the Pharasaic tradition one year. (We got a new perspective on the Pharisees from that provided by the New Testament.) The next year another rabbi gave us a course on the thought of Martin Buber. Claude Welch, chairman of the Department of Religious Thought at the University of Pennsylvania, whose family belongs to our congregation, has generously taught courses for us virtually every year on contemporary theology, comparative religions, etc. An English professor among us has given excellent courses on poetry and literature; and an architect, on art. We try to expose our people to professional teachers of as wide denominational and religious heritage as possible, requiring study of assigned texts in preparation for the weekly classes.

D. *The Ecumenical Institute* (see p. 54), in the fall of 1967, provided an ecumenical context for study of major social issues. The Institute grew out of a course in the winter of 1966-67 on Black Power/White Power participated in by four congregations in northwest Philadelphia—two Episcopal, one Methodist, one Jewish. It was learned that together we could expose our people to the problems of our metropolitan area more competently and more fruitfully than we could as individual congregations. It is hoped that much of our study and action regarding national, metropolitan and local community issues will be done ecumenically in the future.

E. *The Church Bookstore* merits mention as an effective

way of bringing books to the congregation in the context of
the coffee hour in our social hall following Sunday morning
worship. At this coffee hour we give away coffee and sell
books. The key is availability. If a book is reviewed in the
church newsletter, mentioned in the sermon, and available at
the coffee hour, some copies of it will be sold that day. Study
groups are encouraged to purchase their books through the
Bookstore on Sunday morning, making a lively and interesting
crowd around the book table. Some books have had a wide
reading: Robinson's *Honest to God*, for example, was bought
by more than one hundred fifty of our people. We encourage
our people to buy books as well as to borrow them. Encouraging the congregation to read books relevant to our work in
the church and the world is a very useful way of broadening
their awareness of what's going on outside our own limited environment. It is a way of enabling the people to share the current insights and experiences of others struggling with the
same issues, and to realize that other people and other congregations are also in ferment. It is a way, also, of forcing the
clergy to keep as up-to-date in their reading as some of the lay
persons. In time it is possible to assume wide congregational
acquaintance with new movements and concepts. The congregation develops a kind of language perculiar to its own
experience and expressive of its own unique flavor, in which
words and phrases such as "Zorba," "the zoo story,"
"Shalom," "koinonia," "laughers and listmakers," "diakonia,"
"sin on bravely," "honest to God," "Heloise," "secular city"
evoke their own constellation of memory and meaning. So by
means of books, classes, study groups, and lectionary, the
congregation is exposed to the Word that comes to us in the
gospel and in the world.

The Priesthood

It is a mystery how the warp and woof of the congregations' life is interwoven, and how the hundreds of individual
strands combine to make a strangely moving tapestry of

humanity. Trying to dissect this mystery is as fruitless as try-ing to discern a man's spirit from a photograph of him. Yet there are some visible features of the congregation's life that enable or embody its life of mutual priesthood.

The coffee hour is not to be taken lightly. It is a family-style "happening" in our social hall which consists of scores of conversations, looking at the paintings or photographs on the walls that week, sermon discussions, book buying, waving to friends across the hall, running into your friends' children or being run into by them, rump meetings—i.e., fellowship. Some people cannot stand the noisy conviviality, but for many of us, and especially for strangers among us, the coffee hour is the congregational family in stereo. Just as you can usually get the "feel" of a family when you spend an hour or so around their table; so you can get the "feel" of our congre-gation at a typical coffee hour. A man who had moved to Philadelphia, whose family had not yet joined him, com-mented on what he found in the coffee hour.

It came as something of a shock to me one Sunday morning at 11:15 A.M. to realize that I had not yet spoken a single word. When I opened my mouth to join in the singing of a hymn and nothing came out, I began to retrace my steps. My day had gone like this: I awakened in my garret room, washed, dressed, and left the rooming house without seeing anyone. The streets were almost empty, and I entered the subway at an automatic turnstyle, secur-ing a transfer from a machine. The subway and trolley rides were completely impersonal—many people alone in the midst of a crowd—and since I arrived at church a few minutes late, there was no one to greet me at the door, and I took my seat silently. Aside from nodding to the usher, I had no personal contact with anyone that day until the coffee-hour time following the service. I never valued coffee more, nor quite realized the value of this time of fellowship to people in my condition.[7]

Tidings, our weekly newsletter, is a virtually indispensable vehicle for enabling our congregational priesthood. Witty, chatty, informal on mimeographed paper, written since its first issue more than six years ago by a woman who knows and loves the congregation and has a rare gift of insight and expression, *Tidings* tells us each week whom to cry with and whom to rejoice with, whom to pray for, what's happened and what's going to happen. People who think nothing about missing Sunday morning worship avidly read *Tidings*. The latest copy of *Tidings* is a stock item to be found on the bedtables of people in the hospital. While it serves promotional, organizational, ministerial and other ends, its deepest meaning is that it is a family letter circulated among us every week. Its value in enabling and expressing the congregational priesthood, in my judgment, can scarcely be over emphasized.

For three years now we have prepared a *Lenten Daily Readings* booklet, consisting of forty pages prepared by forty of our people. Many of us, who do not normally read any devotional booklet on a consistent basis, find ourselves reading this booklet day by day in order to see just what friends and strangers in the congregation have to say. Typically, there will be a paragraph describing a personal experience or expressing an insight, preceded by a verse of Scripture, and followed by a brief prayer. This booklet is a valuable way, every Lent, of gathering some of the fruits of the life of our people and sharing them. In this booklet pietists and secularists among us are enabled to "hear" one another and to share one another's deepest convictions and insights.

Retreats provide priceless opportunities for cross-fertilizing the congregation with diverse insight and experience in an intensive weekend context. Young and old, married and single, pietist and secularist can be brought together for common study, discussion, silence, work, recreation, eating and drinking, worship. On Friday night a group of acquaintances will begin their tentative exploration of ideas together. By Sunday morning a group of friends will have shaped their own service of worship, including a composite "sermon" in which each person will give his own insight into the meaning of a biblical passage they have studied together, and concluding with a celebration of the Lord's Supper as honest, simple, profound, and eloquent as the life that has been given and found that weekend. A trivial and funny incident will serve to illustrate how we are rebuked, challenged, and have our images broken by the diversity embodied among us. On one retreat of couples some one suggested that we do some singing after supper, and proposed as a starter, "Carry Me Back to Ole Virginny." Whereupon one of the Negro men present smiled broadly but pointedly at the first man and said, "Carry you back to ole Virginny!"

Mention should also be made of the Woman's Society of Christian Service, Senior Citizens (a group of men who meet monthly for luncheon and a program in our church, ecumenical in composition, now numbering 143 men of 12 denominations), Greentree (young couples and singles' social group), and Tower (older couples and singles' social group). Large numbers of our people find both their deepest friendships and their most significant opportunities to participate in the mission of the congregation through these and other organizations. Persons working together for many years on one of the committees or commissions of the congregation may be bound to one another in rewarding ways. We do not know, and thus cannot chart, all the ways whereby the Holy Spirit is weaving our lives together in the congregation. But we do know that in Sunday morning worship there are times when we know that we belong to each other.

The Third Action Which Must Be Taken to Enable the Congregation to Become a Covenant Community Is to Re-form the Congregational Worship

Liturgy is the celebration of life. Where there is little or no authentic congregational life, the most beautiful liturgy is as appalling and ludicrous as the reading of the wedding service without the wedding party present. Such was my feeling several years ago upon hearing evensong in an exquisite Anglican cathedral, when the small paid choir singing the ancient chants was larger than the congregation. Conversely, where there is authentic congregational life, where people are being called into the convenant and sent forth as secular evangelists, the life of God in our midst breaks out of the ancient liturgy and will not be held within the old forms. The worship service becomes a "happening," something alive, an event which can be shocking and glorious. I used to believe in the early years of my ministry that the most significant events of our congregational life happened elsewhere than in Sunday morning worship: i.e., in the small groups where the covenant became real to us, and in mission groups and personal service where evangelism took place. But in recent years, I have come to realize that the congregational celebration on Sunday can be the deepest and most profoundly real and moving event of the week. It is very difficult to describe why and just how this may be so. It is more to be apprehended than comprehended; more to be caught up in than to observe. But there are times in the congregational celebration when we feel the power and the glory of God moving in our midst.

Many of us felt it when our late Minister of Music, Lawrence Curry, would stop playing the organ during one of the verses of the hymn before the sermon, allowing the congregation to sing a capella. He had trained us to sing without him, a truth which we were to discover most deeply after he died. It was fun watching a guest preacher during that middle hymn. The visitor would look quickly with apprehension at the organ console to see what had happened. Then he would become aware of the choir singing powerfully, unconcerned about the organ's silence, and as he heard how the congregation sang with renewed vigor, he would smile and begin to sing more lustily himself. The same exhilaration is felt now when our present organist and choir director, Michael Korn, moves up a register each verse in the singing of a hymn. We all look forward to those occasions, after the choir has processed into the chancel, when they sing a descant as the congregation sings the last verse of the hymn. As one man put it, "When the choir sings a descant, you could scrape me off the ceiling!" A singing congregation is a joy and a wonder.

I feel the poignant burden-bearing of our congregation sometimes on a Sunday when I see the faces of the people, the beloved faces, and know something of the sorrow or the hope in their hearts. Sometimes a couple will be sitting side by side who have betrayed each other, almost destroyed each other, and yet there they are, testifying by their very presence to the hope of the gospel that they may be forgiven and even reconciled. Sometimes I want to change the opening words of the Invitation to Communion from "all you who are in love and charity with your neighbors" to "all you who want to be in love and charity with your neighbors"—and sometimes I do change those words. There is a heartbreaking longing in the congregation, a life-and-death struggle in this person, a devastating disappointment in that family, a glorious fullfillment in another. How should it be so? Why should it be this way for one and that way for another? What compassion the good shepherd must have for all his sheep, and especially the lost ones, the wounded ones. There is nothing like a congregation of people pouring out their mute and hidden need to God in song and prayer and listening—and sometimes, filled with forgiveness, being stood upon their feet again able to walk out into the world with their heads up.

Sometimes Communion is an event of burning relevance. On July 30, 1967, the Sunday after the riots in American cities, we were to have Communion. The text was I Corinthians 11:23-32: "For I received from the Lord what I also delivered to you, that the Lord Jesus on the night when he was betrayed took bread, and when he had given thanks, he broke it, and said, 'This is my body which is for you. . . .'" The sermon asked the question, "Who is responsible for the riots?" And we were given the picture of Jesus standing in the ghetto among the least of his and our brothers, and spreading his hands out to them, saying: "This is my body." It became clear in fact and in feeling that we were responsible, white America was responsible, for the riots. At the end of the sermon, it was said, "Here on this table is a broken and bleeding body. There in the ghettos of Newark and Detroit and Philadelphia is a broken and bleeding body. It is the same body. He who eats the one without seeking in every way open to him to heal the other, profanes the body of the Lord." Communion was real that day, dangerous, hopeful.[8]

Sometimes Communion joins heaven and earth in bonds of belonging that sound with the deep certainty of Paul's affirmation: "I am convinced that neither death, nor life, nor anything else in all creation, will be able to separate us from the love of God in Christ Jesus our Lord" (Rom. 8:38-39, NEB). The Sunday after our beloved friend and Minister of Music, W. Lawrence Curry, died, Communion had been scheduled. It was as if his death had opened heaven's door to us a little, and "all the company of heaven" were almost tangibly present "The cloud of witnesses" and "the communion of the saints," those ancient phrases, took flesh and blood among us, and for a moment, time and eternity clasped hands. So liturgy is the celebration of our living and dying and living again.

There Is a Twofold Reformation Needed in Our Worship

First, the Worship Must Become a Missionary Celebration

What is the feel and movement of the worship of a missionary congregation? Consider what would be the order and content of a service of worship modeled on I Peter 2:9-10: "But you are a chosen race, a royal priesthood, a holy nation, God's own people, that you may declare the wonderful deeds

of him who called you out of darkness into his marvelous
light. Once you were no people but now you are God's people;
once you have not received mercy, but now you have received
mercy."

The basic movements are those of *calling* and *sending*. We
are called out of darkness into his marvelous light: the corporate prayer of confession is the acknowledgment that God
is even now calling us out of the darkness of our sins and the
sins of the whole world into the light of his forgiveness and
freedom. Once we were no people, but now at this very moment we are made his people; once we had not received
mercy, but now at this very moment we receive his mercy.
He heals the convenant we had broken. We are called in
order that we may be sent, sent forth into the world to declare
the marvelous deeds. There is a missionary thrust and urgency
in the celebration. The litany of consecration, prepared years
ago by Ted Loder, is the acknowledgment that God is even
now sending us into this flesh-and-blood world to do the work
of secular evangelism. Laymen bring forth the offerings of the
people after the sermon, as response to the Word preached
and celebrated all through the service. A layman leads in the
litany of consecration:

Leader: Our Father, to the obedient service of thy kingdom
of justice and peace,

People: We consecrate our gifts and our lives.

Leader: To preach good news to the poor, release to the captives, recovery of sight to the blind,

People: We consecrate our gifts and our lives.

Leader: To the ministry of reconciliation, to healing the sick,
teaching the young, caring for the least of thy children,

People: We consecrate our gifts and our lives. Pour out thy
Spirit upon us that in all thou hast given us we may glorify thee,
through Jesus Christ our Lord, Amen.[9]

It is amazing that Sunday after Sunday one or another line of this litany will underscore the thrust of the sermon that day. Somehow it truly sums up our offering to God and his commission to us. The litany seems as fresh and vital and relevant today as when we first began to use it five years ago.

Second, the Worship Must Become a Secular Celebration

The secularity of our celebration is expressed in the use of contemporary, man-on-the-street language in creed, prayer, and sermon. We use the United Church of Christ creed most of the year because of its vivid, modern language. This creed also uses the present tense to describe the deeds of God who "*calls* the worlds into being, *sets* before us the ways of life and death, etc." (God is alive!) We use the Apostles' Creed and other creeds from time to time to demonstrate our solidarity with the community of faith from its beginnings.

We use "You" in pastoral prayers more often than "Thee" and "Thou." "You" language is more direct, immediate, and real to secular men. Revised Roman Catholic liturgy acknowledges this fact in its use of "You" in reference to God. We continue to use the great collects and chants of the church, again acknowledging our solidarity with the community of faith through all its history.

We have trouble with hymns. Many of the familiar hymns have an antiworld tone, or communicate an escapist, private salvation theology. One of dozens of examples that could be cited is the verse in the hymn, "Beneath the Cross of Jesus" —"content to let the world go by." When we subject the best-known and loved hymns of the congregation to secular screening, many of them are discovered to be, in theological terms, hindrance rather than help. So we find ourselves singing a few hymns very often and wishing somebody would write first-class contemporary hymns as well as creeds, prayers, and sermons.

The secularity of our celebration is expressed in terms of

response to secular events in prayer and sermon. In our prayers, specific mention will be made of recent events in the life of the nation or the congregation. Sometimes names will be named: as when we pray for Ho Chi Minh (we are called to pray for our enemies) and President Lyndon B. Johnson to make peace in Vietnam, as when we thank God for the life of Carl Sandburg (the Sunday after he died), as when we pray for our riot-torn cities (during those weeks), as when we pray for our own healing in time of congregational division or sadness. The more specific and concrete our prayers and our sermons, the more honest and effective they will be.

When the riots exploded in American cities during the summer of 1967, the President asked the nation to gather on Sunday, July 30, to pray for reconciliation. On that Sunday I think it would have been immoral for the sermon to deal with any other subject than the riots because *that* is what had happened to us as a nation the previous weeks. The people came to worship, asking, Is there any Word from the Lord on the riots? The preacher may or may not be able to hear a word from the Lord, he may well confuse the Lord's Word with his own, but he has the obligation to try to hear the Word of the Lord and to communicate it to the people. Nothing would have been more unfaithful to a minister's calling that Sunday than to fiddle with other subjects while American cities were burning. This is not to suggest that every Sunday, sermons should deal with national or local events, but they should when these events are of critical or immediate significance. This means that sermons should be "dated" and will be dated. Sermons are not prepared to be read months or years after the event, but to be heard and acted upon at that particular time and in that particular place. Karl Barth was right when he said that the preacher should hold the Bible in one hand and the daily newspaper in the other.

The way a congregation celebrates the great festivals of the church year is a revelation of who they are. For example, we do not know what do do with Lent. In 1967, because Lent came early that year (Ash Wednesday was February 8) and also because the congregation was preoccupied with preparing for the April Arts Festival, we "lost" Lent. It just slipped by us. Presumably we will find it again in 1968, but maybe not. We have tried congregational suppers followed by either worship services or lecture-discussions, with our own ministers or with visiting "headliners." Whatever we do, a fraction of our people (the same faithful fraction), turns out. Attendance at the Maundy Thursday Communion service has steadily declined over a six-year period. Should we worry about it? Should we continue to hope that a large proportion of the congregation can be encouraged to participate in the Lenten pilgrimage of penitence? Or should we face the fact that most people do not like to be penitent at that or any time of the year, and be content to work with the few who find Lenten observance meaningful? Or, is the basic issue the fact that Lent in particular (and the church calendar in general) no longer makes much dent in the secular calendar of most of our people? If we let the world shape our agenda and fill in our calendar, how do we continue to celebrate our particular history as the people of God within the larger history of the world? Is it important to continue to celebrate our own history? I think it is. I think it is part of the essential ongoing process of rediscovering our roots and being nourished by them as we go about the job of taking our congregational walls down. After all, we are to be *salt* of the earth, not just earth, and *leaven* of the lump, not just lump. So we will keep searching for a more effective celebration of Lent.

But while Lenten celebration seems to be waning (the midweek celebration, that is; Sunday morning attendance continues to be higher than at any other time of the year), the celebration of Pentecost is waxing mightily. Perhaps we find the pentecostal spirit more congenial than the penitential. We would rather have a party than go to the mourner's bench. In any case, we in our congregation love Pentecost. For years we have sought to highlight this third great Christian festival after Christmas and Easter. Perhaps because it has less often been acknowledged as a festival event in the church, we have felt freer to experiment with the service. For several years we celebrated all of Pentecost on one Sunday. Acts 2 was the basis of the sermon. Persons were baptized and new members were received (Acts 2:41), and communion was shared (Acts 2:42). We held no first service on Pentecost, but welcomed all the congregation and Sunday school children and youth to worship together. It was a grand celebration of the birth of the church.

In 1965, an expecially provocative and, to some of our people, disturbing Pentecost service was held. The service opened with folk music piped into the sanctuary from a tape recorder. You could almost see the hair of some people standing on end, and the feet of some other people beginning to tap. Then, as the first day of Pentecost was being described, seven people stood up in the congregation unannounced, and walked, one at a time, forward to the chancel—to the consternation and delight of the congregation. They sat on stools arranged in the chancel. In response to the questioning of the preacher, each began, in turn, to speak the gospel in his own language, i.e., as he understood it in the context of his own life. An insurance executive, a housewife, a real-estate salesman, a student, a teacher, a retired businessman, and a professional photographer spoke with humor and honesty, each out of the problems and in the language of his vocational context. There was a sense of excitement in the congregation, almost of uneasiness. You could not tell who was going to talk when or what was going to happen next. Some people were smiling, some were frowning, a couple walked out. The Communion which followed was exuberant, almost gay in mood.

The congregational response to the service was definitely

"those for" and "those against." Some people were shocked by the piped-in folk music, which took them by surprise, and the words of which were not clear enough to be understood. These people could not see the point of the music. Others were offended by what they regarded as boisterous and irreverent activity in the chancel. Others were upset by what they felt was an inappropriately lighthearted celebration of Communion. But on the other hand, Pentecost "broke through" for some people in that service. The relevance of the biblical world and word was ingeniously appropriate and vivid. Many really "felt" Pentecost as the happening it is meant to be.

In retrospect, it was realized that inadequate preparation and interpretation of the service had been given to the people. There was some truth to the charge that the clergy and a few laymen had slipped something over on them, and had deliberately tried to shock them. The matter of shocking a congregation is ambiguous. Sometimes we ministers want to shock people just to show how "gutsy" or avant-gard or unpious we are. But sometimes shock is a valid technique of breaking through the glazed congregational face and the stained-glass voice of the preacher. One Sunday, the word "whore" was used instead of "prostitute" in the Gospel story of the woman who was a sinner (Luke 7:36), in order to demonstrate (by the offense we felt when the word was used) the offense Simon felt when Jesus talked with the woman. Each situation is different; respect for the sensitivities of others, discretion, taste, and a feeling for what is to be gained and lost are in the mix. We have learned, however, that we need to let the congregation in on our novel worship ideas, not to take them by surprise, but to let the new celebrations be congregational experiments instead of just the experiments of a few.

In addition we have begun to experience our Pentecost Communion as a glad and joyous event. It was hard for many of us, brought up to regard Communion as *always* a solemn and penitential service, to be able to rejoice in the Communion service. And yet, the early church worshiped and celebrated the Lord's Supper on Sunday precisely because it was resurrection day, a day to celebrate the good news of God's victory over sin and death through the death and resurrection of Jesus. Perhaps the centuries have wrongly stressed the Good Friday dimension of Communion to the detriment of the Easter dimension. While it is appropriate to celebrate Communion in a penitential mood during Lent, it is equally appropriate to celebrate it joyously on Pentecost. So this is what we are doing.[10]

In 1966, it was decided that we needed a whole week and two Sundays to celebrate Pentecost thoroughly. So persons were baptized and received into membership one Sunday and Communion shared the next. In 1967, the youth membership class decided that they wanted to get into the act (Acts!) too. As part of membership preparation, they worked on a secret project called "Project Pentecost," prepared their own Pentecost service to be celebrated on Pentecost Sunday prior to the congregational celebration, and invited the congregation to join them (see page 56). As the climax to the service "Project Pentecost" was unveiled. It was a cardboard model of our church's entire building planted squarely on a map of Germantown. The roof was off so that you could see everything, and the major surprise was that the walls of the sanctuary fell open to the streets and people of Germantown. It was a model of The Church Inside Out,[11] a congregation without walls, but with roots.

One day George McLeod, pastor of a church located on High Street in Glasgow, Scotland, chanced to look up at the stained glass windows over the chancel of the sanctuary. The phrase "Glory to God in the Highest" was carved in the glass. As he looked he noticed that a pane of glass was broken and missing, the pane on which the letter "e" in the word "highest" was carved. Suddenly he found himself seeing the words that were now there, "Glory to God in the High st." And it struck him that the only way to glorify God in the *highest* is to glorify him in the *High St.*

Perhaps it is because our church building is located at the corner of Germantown Avenue and High St. that this story is so pertinent to our congregation. But perhaps it is pertinent to you and your congregation as well.

People who worship are people who pray, or want to pray.

SECULAR PRAYER

ON ASH WEDNESDAY in 1966 I conducted a Day of Prayer at Union Theological Seminary. Two weeks before the day, the following comment of a Union student was relayed to me: "Don't you think it is irrelevant—a Day of Prayer when things like Vietnam are going on? I feel like I'm dragging around a useless God-hypothesis. Where is God in all this?" Many Christians share with that student the two major objections to prayer raised by today's secular man: (1) Doubt that there is a personal God to whom to pray. (2) Suspicion that, even if there is, prayer is irrelevant to what is going on in the world. Abraham J. Heschel defines the doubt when he says that the crisis of prayer today is a crisis of theology. "If God is a what, a power, the sum total of values, how can we pray to an it? An 'I' does not pray to an 'it.' Unless, therefore, God is at least as real as my own self; unless I am sure that God has at least as much life as I do, how can I pray?"[1] Doubt concerning the nature of God cripples prayer.

We have to respect this doubt because in one form or another we all share it at times. A few may take the position of Christian atheism, as exemplified by Thomas J. J. Altizer and William Hamilton, among others. For Christian atheists, prayer would seem to be utterly without meaning and futile.[2] Indeed, if God is dead, whether he died recently or when Jesus was born, or never existed, prayer in the sense of any personal relationship with God today would be meaningless. We do not pray to a nonexistent deity or to the good-in-ourselves, or to whomever it may concern (A man's anguished

109

soliloquy under a seeming deaf and silent sky, may, however, be a profound prayer under some other name.[3]

Others may take the position of Christian agnosticism, as exemplified today by increasing numbers of laity and clergy. For Christian agnostics, God is not dead (for how would we know if he were?). The word "God" is dead. The word "God" has no content, so we must remain silent when asked questions about God, ultimate reality or being, and point to Jesus as the one in whom we meet "God." Prayer becomes "reflection upon the situation in the light of the Christian perspective and leads to appropriate action."[4]

Most Christians today are Christian-atheist-believers. We are "I believe, help my unbelief" (Mark 9:24) men, men who want to pray, but who cannot quite bring it off, cannot find handles to grab onto. A friend of mine said, "I'm hung up on prayer." He said it with a certain anguish, a knowledge that there is reality in prayer, a reality that eludes him, an acknowledgment that there is something he's missing or has lost. This man does not regard prayer as a trivial matter, to be mocked or made light of or ignored. He wants to pray but does not know how, or quite why and may in his passionate uncertainty be closer to the heart of prayer than he realizes (Rom. 8:26). This man wants a way to God, and the way will have to lead through the neighbor. "Heart speaks to heart, and this may well be God's dialogue with man."[5] Secular man believes that if he can meet God at all, he will meet Him in the neighbor.

The images of God today are confused and confusing. We engage in a vast theological shell game, looking first under this shell and then under that. Not finding God, we finally realize that he is not under any shell or caught in any image, that he is not a man in the sky or a blob of protoplasm in the ground, or the yeast of history. We need perspective on our God imagery. Neither height imagery nor depth imagery nor any other kind of imagery can separate us from or adequately describe, the God who is in Jesus Christ. No image is wholly adequate; some images are more helpful than others. Christians must take seriously prevailing New Testament imagery. Paul writes, "He [Christ] is the image of the invisible God" (Col. 1:15). John writes, "He who has seen me has seen the Father" (John 14:9). The witness of the New Testament is that when we look into the humanity of Jesus, we are looking into the mystery of God.

When Jesus prayed he spoke to God as *Father*. Gunther Bornkamm explains the meaning of Jesus' lips of the term "Father."

> The nearness of God is the secret of Jesus' language about God as Father. This is . . . shown in the expression by which Jesus chooses to address God in prayer, an expression which would have appeared to any Jew too unceremonious and lacking in respect. *Abba-Father*, this is the word Jesus uses (Mark 14:36) and which the Hellenistic Church has taken over in its original Aramaic from the oldest records about Jesus (Romans 8:15; Galatians 4:6). It is the child's familiar address to his father here on earth, completely unknown in religious language. The nearness of the Father in his Goodness certainly does not exclude the majesty of God, the demanding King (Matthew 12:50), and the Judge to come (Matthew 10:33; 16:27). This corresponds with the address "Our Father—who are in heaven" (Matthew 6:9), in the prayer which Jesus teaches his disciples, and in which both trust and reverence are embraced.[6]

If ultimate reality at its deepest is personal[7] (as the prophets, psalmists, and Jesus believed) then the term "Father" may be less inadequate than any other to speak of God.

The second objection to prayer is the suspicion that prayer is irrelevant to what is going on in the world. Irrelevant in the sense that it is not efficacious, that it does not move the arm of God, that it does not exert power on action or event. Paul Tillich responds to our skepticism.

God's directing creativity is the answer to the question of the meaning of prayer, especially prayers of supplication and prayers of intercession. Neither type of prayer can mean that God is expected to acquiesce in interfering with existential conditions. Both mean that God is asked to direct the given situation toward fulfillment. The prayers are an element in this situation, a most powerful factor if they are true prayers. As an element in the situation, a prayer is a condition of God's directing creativity, but the form of this creativity may be the complete rejection of the manifest content of the prayer. Nevertheless, the prayer may be heard for its hidden content, which is the surrender offering of a fragment of existence to God. This hidden content is decisive. It is the element of the situation which is used by God's directing creativity. Every serious prayer contains power, not because of the intensity of desire expressed in it but because of the faith the person has in God's directing activity—a faith which transforms the existential situation.[8]

We shall explore later in the chapter the hidden content of prayer, the surrender offering of our fragments of existence to God. For the moment let us acknowledge that Tillich's statement, profound as it is, is still an affirmation of his own faith. There are no satisfying "answers" to our skepticism about the efficacy of prayer. In prayer, as in every other dimension of Christian life, we have to go out not knowing, without guarantee or guidebook. The only way to find out if there is meaning in prayer is to pray.

Some prayers are an escape from responsibility, a cover for disobedience, a substitute for things we should be doing instead of waiting for God to do them. Isaiah blasts such dubious devotions with a burning mandate for the kind of prayer and fasting that are acceptable to God.

> Is not this the fast that I choose;
>   to loose the bonds of wickedness,
>   to undo the thongs of the yoke,
>   to let the oppressed go free,
>   and to break every yoke?

Is it not to share your bread with the hungry,
    and bring the homeless poor into your house;
    when you see the naked, to cover him,
    and not to hide yourself from your own flesh?
Then shall your light break forth like the dawn,
    and your healing shall spring up speedily;
    your righteousness shall go before you,
    and the glory of the Lord shall be your rear guard.
Then you shall call, and the Lord will answer;
    you shall cry, and he will say, Here I am.
                  Isaiah 58:6-9 (italics added)

So let us affirm unequivocally *with* secular man that prayer *is bound to mission*.[9] Prayer and mission are two sides of the coin of the kingdom. We cannot legitimately pray for peace in Vietnam unless we are offering ourselves to do and say whatever we can to bring peace in Vietnam, and in our own city, and in our own family. We cannot legitimately pray for the poor unless we are working to change those political and economic structures of society that *keep* people poor. We cannot legitimately pray for an individual unless we are willing to make ourselves available to do whatever God would call us to do in relation to that individual. We cannot ask God to forgive us if we are not willing to forgive our brothers ("If you are . . . at the altar, and there remember that your brother has something against you, leave your gift there before the altar and go; first be reconciled to your brother, and then come" (Matt. 5:23-24). The altar is in the world, as Pope Paul VI celebrated the Mass in Yankee Stadium. Our prayer has to square with our life, what we say to God with what we do to and for our neighbor. Heschel says, ". . . a man's prayer is answered only if he stakes his very life on it."[10] This kind of prayer is not trying to move the arm of God, but seeks instead to make us available to be moved by God for his purposes.

Let us also affirm unequivocally *to* secular man that *mission is bound to prayer*. Christian mission require both

discernment and commitment. Discernment without commitment is hypocrisy. Commitment without discernment is
fanaticism. If pietists have often been guilty of hypocrisy,
secularists are often quilty of fanaticism. Discernment is not
guaranteed. We cannot baptize all change as God's doing or
identify our convictions with the will of God.

Where does the *gift* of discernment come from? When,
where, how, and to whom does it come? Paul suggests that
every congregation is called to be a community of discernment (Eph. 1:18; Phil. 1:9-11; Rom. 12:1-2). Any theology,
new or old, which suggests that we can faithfully participate
in secular evangelism without faithful participation in some
form of the covenant community, is defective and unbiblical.
How are we to recognize the incognito Christ at work in the
world unless he reveals himself to us in our life together? How
can we be authentic signposts unless we are also signs, sinful
signs as we are?

"Wrestle and pray," wrote Paul (Eph. 6:12, 18, KJV). Real
involvement in the lives and events of our times drives us to
acknowledge the limits of our vision and our inability to love
our friends, let alone our enemies. Such involvement drives us
to worship and pray, not as some religious duty but as men
who know they are dying and crave life, as men who want to
be healed, men who want to discern and obey. As long as we
cloister ourselves from the conflicts and tensions of the world,
our need of God may remain hidden from us. A priest once
described what it is like to hear the confession of nuns. He
said, "It's like being stoned to death with popcorn."[11] When
we are radically involved in the sufferings of this world (as
many nuns are) and participate in its brutalities, tragedies,
and failures, our confessions will consist of rocks and our sins
will be heavy and dark. We will discover our need of God as
never before, a need for that worship which "disinfects the
ego,"[12] that Word which judges and saves, that prayer which
makes men whole and holy. Secular man's cardinal text for
prayer is Romans 8:26: ". . . for we do not know how to pray

as we ought, but the Spirit himself intercedes for us with sighs too deep for words." Prayer is that inarticulate groaning, that longing too deep for words, which rises out of the depths of our living. This is prayer that will be brief, direct, honest, and with a place for silent hoping.

One of the striking, and often unacknowledged, dimensions of Dietrich Bonhoeffer, the "father" of many secular Christians, is precisely his unashamed, authentic piety. He was a secular man who prayed. Jesus was a secular man who prayed, one who took great pains to teach his followers to pray. We may note that the generations alternate: the fathers were tempted to be holier-than-thou, the sons are tempted to be worldlier-than-thou. The sons, secular men, would much rather be wise as serpents than innocent as doves, and do not want to be a fool for anybody's sake. We are more at home in the world than in the church. So when we consider the church, we prefer to discuss its mission rather than its nature. When we consider Jesus, we are more comfortable with his humanity than his mystery. When we consider morality, we prefer to begin with context rather than content. When we consider prayer, we would rather begin with *prayer-on-location*, prayer in the midst, on the run than *prayer-in-reflection*, prayer that happens off-location in a time and place of solitude or rest.

A simple definition of prayer may guide our exploration. Prayer is awareness of the response to God who addresses us in the world and in the gospel.[13] The abiding polarities of prayer are world and gospel. Awareness/response to God addressing us in the gospel is *prayer-in-reflection*, "chronos" prayer. Awareness/response to God addressing us in the world is *prayer-on-location*, "kairos" prayer.[14]

Prayer-on-Location

Prayer-on-location begins with the awareness that God is present in all things,[15] events, and persons. The risen Christ came to his disciples at first incognito, as a stranger on the beach, in the garden, in the upper room, on the road to Emmaus. In Matthew 25:31 ff., we are given the clue as to where he will reveal himself to us now, namely in "the least of these" whom we either serve or do not serve. He is there today in the humble powerless ones. We are to look for his face in the faces of human need. Christians are those who recognize and acknowledge him wherever in the world walls of hostility are being broken down and human need served. Awareness of Christ's living presence (God is alive!) means that Christian prayer is always Easter prayer, not in mood but in derivation. Even our "Gethsemane" and "Cross" prayers are Easter prayers in the sense that the Spirit prays with us, in us, and despite us, ever shaking and enlivening us (Rom. 8:1-11). Thus Easter language, i.e., Christ-language ("I am with you always, Matt. 28:20) may be preferable to God-language. The indicative of prayer-on-location is awareness of Christ's living presence in all things, events, persons.

This risen incognito Christ is manifestly alive, ambulatory, on the move. Prayer to the Lord on the move will therefore not be static but dynamic, spontaneous, free-wheeling. Malcolm Boyd gets this in-flight imagery in the title and content of his book of prayers, *Are You Running with Me, Jesus?*

It's morning, Jesus. It's morning, and here's that light and sound all over again.

I've got to move fast . . . get into the bathroom, wash up, grab a bite to eat, and run some more.

I just don't feel like it, Lord. What I really want to do is get back into bed, pull up the covers, and sleep. All I seem to want today is the big sleep, and here I've got to run all over again.

Where am I running? You know these things I can't understand. It's not that I need to have you tell me. What counts most is just that somebody knows, and it's you. That helps a lot.

So I'll follow along, okay? But lead, Lord. Now I've got to run. Are you running with me, Jesus?

What counts most is just that somebody knows, and it's you.
That helps a lot.

So I'll follow along, okay? But lead, Lord. Now I've got to run.
Are you running with me, Jesus?[16]

Prayer on the run. It's not really such a new idea after all.
"If I ascend into heaven, thou art there; if I make my bed in
Sheol thou art there. If I take the wings of the morning and
dwell in the uttermost parts of the sea, even there thy hand
shall lead me and they right hand shall hold me" (Ps. 139:8-
10). But it is an especially appealing current idea. It's one
way of putting the theological question: Are you there, Lord?
Are you running, scrambling, crawling, crying, laughing with
me, Jesus?

Many people today find Boyd's "hip" language speaking to
and for them:

I'm crying and shouting inside tonight, Lord, and I'm
feeling completely alone

I'm scared, Jesus. You've asked me to do something
I don't think I can do

In this ugly red building, old people are waiting for
death

I'm having a ball, and I just want to thank you, Jesus

They've been married for twenty years, Jesus, and
they say they hate each other

This young girl got pregnant, Lord, and she isn't
married

Michel Quoist's *Prayers* have remarkable depth and insight
as they too give the taste, smell and feel of the flesh-and-blood
situation of the prayer. His prayer titles include: "The Telephone," "Green Blackboards," "The Wire Fence," "The
Baby," "Posters," "The Subway," "The Swing," "At the
Door," "Prayer before a Twenty-Dollar Bill," "The Porno-
graphic Magazine," "The Tractor," "The Bald Head," "Foot-

ball at Night," "Eyes."[18] These prayers-on-location poignantly describe the raw data of the human situation in the presence of Christ. It is clear that nothing and nowhere can be off-limits for this incognito, ambulatory Christ.[19] We must be on the alert to see and hear him at any time, in any place, event, and person. "Perfect attention is prayer."[20]

Prayer-on-location springs from an awareness of the triadic dimension of all events and relations, the depth dimension. The Spirit of Christ is at work in the world creating a single new humanity, making us aware that we are bound to all men as "soul brothers," making us cry "Abba, Father!" (in secular terms, "Oh, my brother!"). Awareness that Christ lives in my neighbor, though unacknowledged by him, frees me from religious imperialism or proselytism. I am free to regard him as already loved and inhabited by Christ, a person from whom I may learn something new of Christ, one whom I am called to serve and, if it is appropriate, one to whom I may speak of Christ. I am free to look at him as he is, and to welcome him as he comes out of hiding and reveals himself (the image of Christ in him) to me. Prayer is awareness of the potentiality for community which results from Christ's presence in every man and in me.

Such awareness is a gift, not an achievement. It is a special kind of eyesight. Herb Gardner in A Thousand Clowns describes this eyesight in secular coinage which can be cashed by anybody. An uncle tells what he wants for his nephew.

I just want him to stay with me 'til I can be sure he won't turn into a Norman Nothing. I want to be sure he'll know when he's chickening out on himself. I want him to get to know exactly the special thing he is or else he won't notice it when it starts to go. I want him to stay awake and know who the phonies are. I want him to know how to holler and put up an argument, I want a little guts to show before I can let him go. I want to be sure he sees all the wild possibilities. I want him to know it's worth all the trouble just to give the world a little goosing when you get the chance.

And I want him to know the subtle, sneaky, important reason why he was born a human being and not a chair. I will be very sorry to see him go. The kid was the best straight man I ever had. He is a laugher, and laughers are rare. I mean, you tell that kid something funny—not just any piece of corn, but something funny, and he'll give you your money's worth. It's not just funny jokes he reads, or I tell him, that he laughs at. Not just set-up funny stuff. He sees street jokes, he has the good eye, he sees subway farce and cross-town bus humor and all the cartoons people make by being alive. He has a good eye.[21]

That's it, the good eye, the caring capacity to see into the suffering and joy of human beings.[22] The man with the good eye will pray street prayers, not stained-glass prayers; prayers that will be more earthy than heavenly; prayers that laugh and cry. The indicative of prayer-on-location is the awareness that the incognito, ambulatory Christ is present with us in all things, events, and persons.

The imperative of prayer-on-location is *response* to Christ. Response on location. Do you remember the letter mentioned on page 13? "I would hope that we could keep both the baby and the bathwater, doing community organization in slum areas, and in that context developing depth relationships between people, fighting our corrupt magistrates' system [in Philadelphia] and living the life of prayer that will enable us to fight with love towards the magistrates and the bosses who support them, trying to renew the public structures, and being a sign of the kingdom to our neighbor. I cannot believe that the picketers and the pray-ers must forever go their separate ways." That man has taught me something of what it means to lobby, picket, demonstrate and argue prayerfully, to pray without ceasing (Eph. 1:16; 6:18; Rom. 1:9; Col. 1:9). The freedom songs of the civil rights movement are *prayers-on-location*. The moment of danger, passion, confrontation is the moment for these articulate songs or inarticulate groans when deep calls to deep.

When hostility is the greatest and pressure and tension are hottest, we are called to respond with prayer-on-location. In a brief Thanksgiving message taped at a television studio in Philadelphia some years ago, I noted that President Johnson in his Thanksgiving Proclamation asked us to pray for our own men in Vietnam and the South Vietnamese. I said that I wished he had gone on to suggest that we pray as well for the Vietcong and North Vietnamese men. We do have it on good authority that we are to pray for our enemies. After the taping, as I was leaving the studio, a cameraman came up to me and said, "Whaddya mean, pray for the Vietcong. We gotta kill those bastards. In wartime this Christianity stuff has to be put aside so we can get the job done." We talked together for a while, and it developed that the man was a loyal churchman. Only as we pray for enemies, national and personal, can we begin to see them as brothers and not bastards, literally bound to us and we to them by the Spirit in human solidarity, the solidarity of sinners called to be saints. How can we love a man at work who is undermining our job or reputation (love him *while* we are at work with him), or an unfaithful husband or wife *while* we are at home together, or hostile parents and children *when* we are with them, unless in prayer for them on-location we see in the light of Christ our own concrete sinfulness and their potential saintliness? Whom shall we thank for the laughter of children, the love of spouse, the loyalty of friends, the beauty and marvel of sight and sound, the sheer joy of being alive, unless we thank God then and there when gladness rises up on-location. Sometimes we are just happy, and do not feel like thanking anyone in particular. Sometimes we feel fortunate and can thank our lucky stars. Sometimes we are grateful to particular persons who have given or forgiven us much. But sometimes our gratitude ranges higher and deeper. When our son was born, I was grateful to my wife, and to the doctor and nurses. But this was not enough. For the child was a gift to both me and my wife,

a gracious gift from Life. So I had to, and wanted to, thank
the God of all life. Such prayers of praise will be leaping and
dancing prayers (2 Sam. 6:16; Acts 3:8), "Zorba" prayers.[23] Many such prayers today will celebrate the marvels of
God's creative work in addition to his saving work.

Such prayers-on-location will be brief, direct, immediate,
spontaneous, often silent, rising out of the anguish or joy of
the moment. When you see the hostile one, "Brother Saul,
brother George." When joy takes you by surprise, "Thank
you, Lord!" When you see the suffering, deceit, longing,
loneliness, hope of another, "God bless you." "Christ, have
mercy on Bob, Sue." When under pressure, "Lord, help me,"
"strengthen me," "forgive me," "deliver me." It is said that
Martin Luther, when he became afraid or uncertain, would
pray, "I am baptized; I am baptized," reminding himself who
he was and whose he was, and that the hand of Christ was
irrevocably on him no matter what.

Some prayers will have humor and irony, such as those in
Prayers from the Ark.[25] The Tortoise prays:

> A little patience,
> O God,
> I am coming.
> One must take nature as she is!
> It was not I who made her!
> I do not mean to criticize
>   this house on my back—
>   it has its points—
>   but You must admit, Lord,
>   it is heavy to carry!
> Still,
>   let us hope that this double enclosure,
>   my shell and my heart,
>   will never be quite shut to You.

Some prayers will be "sin on bravely" prayers, moving in their
honesty and faith. Such is the prayer of Dimitri Karamazov

from the depths of his own willful degradation: "For I am a Karamazov. For when I do leap into the pit, I go headlong with my heels up, and am pleased to be falling in that degrading attitude, and pride myself upon it. And in the very depths of that degradation I begin a hymn of praise. Let me be accursed. Let me be vile and base, only let me kiss the hem of the veil in which my God is shrouded. Though I may be following the devil, I am thy son, O Lord, and I love Thee, and I feel the joy without which the world cannot stand."[26]

One of Quoist's prayers is titled "Before You, Lord."[27] For me this phrase well sums up the intent and content of prayers-on-location. "Before You, Lord"—in the study, office, street, subway, at the bedside, graveside—always before You, Lord. I find that phrase coming to my mind often. It is a street prayer not a stained-glass prayer. And sometimes it helps me to substantize the "You" by visualizing the crucifix —before You, on your Cross, Lord. In the midst of severe tension or temptation, exaltation or depression, I plant that crucifix in the midst of my situation, between me and the other person or persons. "Here I am, here we are, before you, Lord, before You, on Your Cross."

A man asked a priest how he bore his cross of celibacy. The priest replied, "With great difficulty." Then he pointed to a painting hanging on the wall of his room depicting a man kneeling and looking up at the crucifix. At the bottom of the scene was the legend: "Et maiora sustinuit ipso" (And greater pains than yours has He endured). "That inscription helps," the priest said.[28] May it also help us in our prayers-on-location.

If prayer-on-location is "kairos" prayer, awareness-response to Christ addressing us in the persons and events of the world, then prayer-in-reflection is "chronos" prayer, awareness-response to Christ addressing us in the gospel. In prayer-on-location the weight is on active response to Christ; in prayer-in-reflection the weight is on receptive awareness of Christ.

Prayer-in-Reflection

Prayer-in-reflection usually takes place off-location, in a time and place of solitude, rest, or anonymity (as on a train). It is not, however, irrelevant or escapist. It is, rather, the creative brooding of Moses in the desert where he heard the divine call to go and liberate his enslaved brothers. It is the struggling and searching and deciding of Jesus in the wilderness where he heard the divine call to his specific mission. It is the kind of reflection: which "must not so much mollify as awaken and provoke men and sharpen thought. . . . fetch men up out of the cellar, call to them, turn their comfortable way of thinking topsy-turvy with the dialectic of truth."[29]

Prayer-in-reflection is before and after involvement. It is the quiet, judicious sifting of what has been happening to you, the clear-eyed evaluation of what you have done and become, the time of self-knowledge when the contours of the self become visible. Buber warns us, "Self-knowledge leads a person either to self-destruction or rebirth."[30] Prayer-in-reflection handles this critical self-knowledge. It is the time of healing, realignment, sharpening the good eye, receiving the gift of discernment. It is the time of organizing your thoughts, thinking about your past and future, deciding on the next line of action, calming yourself down, sorting out your priorities. It is the time of being still and knowing, a time not of doing or saying but of being before God.[31]

Is such prayer-in-reflection essential for Christian living, essential for every Christian? Does everyone need such times apart—monthly, weekly, daily? Who is to say? In seminary I remember being shocked when I learned that a revered professor had no regular time for daily prayer. I had been brought up to believe that daily devotions was one of the marks of authentic Christian living. Today I realize that there are many Christians who do not seem to need or want frequent periods of prayer in order to sort out their own lives and to live in harmony with their fellows and the purpose of God. One does remember that Jesus appeared to need times of solitude when he could pray, (Mark 1:35; 14:32; etc.). Are there any men who do not need time for some kind of reflection?

We may well have reversed things in terms of the discipline of daily prayer.[32] Typically we have given seekers very specific rules of prayer. After a week or a month, they have failed to live up to it; it has become law instead of gospel, and they are now bound instead of free. One night while putting one of my daughters to bed, I said it was time for her prayer. She said, "I'm too tired to pray now; besides, I pray during the day at school. God doesn't mind if I don't pray now, does he?" I guess not. . . . Perhaps we should not try to put children or adults on a *schedule* of prayer, but encourage them to pray as the Spirit moves them (as they feel like it) during the day. Then, as our responsibilities get more complex and our lives more confusing, and as the limits of our own understanding and strength become more manifest, *then* we may want times of solitude and quiet for reflection and restoration. (Indeed, I am wary of the man who does not crave some moments and occasions of solitude.) The time of discipline, then, may come well along the way of prayer, when discipline is not experienced as burden but as liberation, enabling us to be what we want and do what we want. As Heschel puts it, we need both "order and outburst, regularity and spontaneity,"[33] but the ordering regularity should follow the spontaneous outburst as the wild horse is disciplined for productive work.

I have become accustomed to a daily time for prayer-in-reflection, though I cannot always get it, and when I cannot, I no longer feel guilty about it (most of the time!). The daily pattern may be useful for those who are able to arrange their day easily for such a period alone. But there are many people for whom an hour or two once a week may be both more feasible and more productive than a few minutes daily. This is a time when we should encourage businessmen, housewives, students, technicians, assembly-line workers, etc., to search out a style of praying which suits the specifics of their own life, a secular rather than a cloister style, shaped around the calendar of their world rather than the calendar of the church.

Prayer-in-reflection begins with *awareness* of the risen Christ coming to us and addressing us in the gospel. Yet before we can truly "hear" the gospel in the first-person, we need as secular men to lay out our world before God. This is the world of our relationships and responsibilities, the things that weigh on our minds and hearts. We do not go apart to pray in order to forget our responsibilities and relationships but to reflect on them. We cannot begin to pray except as we can "unload" all the turmoil inside us, the achievements and satisfactions as well as the resentments and guilt. When we make lists of letters to write, people to telephone, presents to buy, groceries to get, references to look up, orders to make out, we *can* be praying. Every list we make *could* be a prayer list. The on-location data of our lives is the raw material of our prayer. "I am a multitude when I pray," in the words of Abraham J. Heschel. It may be useful for us to sort out our particular multitude, to write down the specific persons and situations in which we would seek God's pardon and promise.

When I have "laid myself out," then I am ready to "hear" the gospel, as it comes to me in the biblical word, the liturgy, an appropriate reading, or the words of friends and enemies. I grew up with a pietist confidence in the biblical word as the earthen vessel par excellence capable of yielding treasures of insight, healing, and power. In recent years I have learned

from Roman Catholic, Orthodox, and Jewish friends the fruitfulness of the liturgy as the distillation of the gospel, and
richly productive of reflective prayer. We need that objective
Word to counter and jolt us, to give us perspective on our
own situation, to judge us and give us hope. The Word provides us with insight and will for the way through and beyond
our own situation.

There are, then, the two polarities of our world and the
gospel, the same Lord coming to us in each, the gospel and
our world now beginning to interrelate, criss-cross, move
back and forth. A process of creative brooding begins, a
pondering, considering, wondering. Out of the particularities
of our world and the particularity of this gospel Word, the
Spirit moves us to pray (see prayer on page 71).

I would raise three additional concerns in the form of questions. First, how can we find a viable context for corporate
prayer between the loneliness of private prayer and the
anonymity of much congregational worship today? It is naïve
to suppose that most people can continue to grow in the practice of prayer-in-reflection by themselves. Prayer on a solo
basis is only for the mature, and even for them, its idiosyncra-
sies and private confusions beg for clarification, rebuke, and
confirmation. It is also naïve to suppose that the worship of
the large congregation is an adequate context for personal
reflection (except when the service is dead and empty). Most
of us need either the individual guidance of a person to whom
we can talk from time to time about our prayer, or the corporate guidance of a small group of persons with whom we
are covenanted to pray. (Again and again our individual
Bible study in preparation for the Covenant Group or
koinonia group meetings produced authentic reflective
prayer. I am convinced that many outside the church will find
meaningful prayer *only* in some such small group, probably
outside the environs of the ecclesiastical milieu itself. Many
inside the church will find a new depth of corporate prayer in

such a group. The function of the small group as enabling both reflective and on-location prayer seems to me of great significance today.)

Second, how can we motivate ourselves and others for that "prayerful reading which is the continuous memory of God?"[34] Heschel says that the words of the liturgy are footholds for the soul and that to pray is to take hold of the word, to follow it, to explore its deeper meaning.[35] How can secular man be encouraged to take the time to take hold of the Word and follow it? In a recent lecture, John Ciardi[36] described the waiting of a poet for the gift of inspiration in Robert Frost's words, as "hanging around words to overhear them whispering to one another." He went on to say that language is wiser than men, and that language shapes men more than men shape language. How shall we, in this word-debasing age, gain new respect for words and attend to the wisdom of language? A Greek Orthodox friend once said, "In our churches, you go to church to enter into the prayer of Christ. . . . Prayer is memorized that it may be sung, and so the liturgy creeps into the bones of the children."[37] That recalled to me the daily family devotions of my childhood when the language of the Psalms did creep into my bones. But if family devotions today are cursory and spasmodic, not a live option for most of us, where shall the words creep into modern men and their children?

Sometimes the words creep in through congregational worship. One summer Sunday, in a little Michigan church, one of our daughters leaned over to her mother during the singing of "*The Church's One Foundation*" and whispered, " 'To be his holy bride' is the line I love, Mom." What that phrase meant to her I am not sure, but that it does mean something real and important to her I do not doubt.

Apart from congregational and family worship, however, how can we encourage people today to meditate, not to speed-read, but to ponder and wonder as they read? The words will not yield instantly any more than the beloved. A certain wooing and waiting are necessary. I am reminded of the story in which Hell is defined as a place where the French are the mechanics, the English the cooks, the Germans the comedians, and the Americans the lovers. Americans may be no better pray-ers than lovers! There is value in reading aloud from time to time so that the words are known by the mouth and the ear as well as by the eye. We are invited to consent to the Word in the words, to behold a text, to suffer it, to rejoice in it, to surrender to it, to be resurrected by it. Sometimes it becomes a dialogue with God; sometimes a duet, when we cooperate with the spirit praying within us: "if someone sings, it is only by singing myself that I hear it."[38] But how are we to interest empirical, pragmatic, secular man to cultivate the art of reflection?

Third, what do we believe about God's purpose for us as individuals within his vast cosmic purpose, and how may we pray in this regard? Secular man wonders how God can have an individual purpose for him in a world of indiscriminate suffering and death. Ecclesiastes wondered; Camus wondered; Jesus wondered.[39] How can we understand Psalm 138: 3,8: "On the day *I* called, thou didst answer *me*, *my* strength of soul thou didst increase . . . the Lord will fulfill his purpose for *me*"? (Italics added.)

Prayer-in-reflection begins with the awareness of Christ addressing us in our concrete situation through the gospel. It continues with our response to him. This response-prayer is not calculated to move the arm of God but, rather, to make ourselves available to him that our arms may be moved by him; it is not in order that we may know him but that we may be made known to him; not that our will be done by him but that his will be done in and through and despite us. Not that he should interfere with the existential situation, but that he may transform it. Reflective prayer is the "surrender offering" of our fragment of existence to God.

We offer the past to God. We offer ourselves as we have been and our world as it has been—everything with thanksgiving (Phil. 4:6). We thank God even for that which has been hard and evil, knowing that he works in our personal and corporate betrayals and tragedies to judge us, comfort us, and make us rely on him who raises the dead (I Cor. 2:11). As we reflect on our past we are able to "hear" the criticism of us made by friends and enemies, criticism which we could not hear in the heat of conflict or self-defense. In the light of grace, we can begin to see our sins and acknowledge our guilt and make confession. A homely illustration. Some time ago under pressure of various kinds I found myself tense, insensitive to the people I worked with, typically late for appointments because too much was crammed into the schedule, and thus making mistakes of judgment in my hurry. I shared my growing concern with my father, who nailed me to the wall with his succinct reply, "It's good that you are learning that being a five-foot blade and trying to cut a six-foot swath isn't heroism but egoism, and a subtle form of atheism."[40]

A friend wrote me on the same matter, "Is there something of a tension in your ministry between 'persons' and 'programs'? It sometimes seems and feels as though you turn people on-and-off. People seem either to fit into your plans and programs or they do not, but they feel the distinction too sharply as to whether and when they do or don't. Your openness and sensitivity to others thus becomes more like clothes than flesh, less real than the words which announce their attributes."

We may be thankful for those who do not withhold the truth from us and enable us, in private reflection, to assess and sift the criticism, accepting that which appears to be valid, discarding that which may emanate from a friend's hostility or hurt, and offering all together with them and ourselves, to God.

We offer our past—the joys, accomplishments and fulfill-

ments, the blessed days and people. We offer them all and
ourselves in the faith that nothing is ultimately destroyed or
lost, nothing is beyond resurrection, and indeed much is already resurrected. Bonhoeffer writes from prison:

> . . . gratitude converts the pangs of memory into a tranquil joy.
> The beauties of the past are not endured as a thorn in the flesh,
> but as a gift precious for its own sake. We must not wallow in
> our memories or surrender to them, just as we don't gaze all the
> time at a valuable present, but get it out from time to time, and
> for the rest hide it away as a treasure we know is there all the
> time. . . . From the moment we awake until we fall asleep we
> must commend our loved ones wholly and unreservedly to God,
> and leave them in his hands, transforming our anxiety for them
> into prayers on their behalf.[41]

So by faith the past is brought into the future.

We offer the future to God. We offer ourselves as we would
be, our friends and enemies as they would be, our world as it
is becoming, everything with thanksgiving. Our prayers go
before and beyond all that we can do and say; they reach
through our hope and take the flesh of waiting like watchmen
for the morning. Jesus said to Peter, "I have prayed for you
that your faith may not fail; and when you have turned again,
strengthen your brethren" (Luke 22:32). Peter could never
forget Jesus' prayer when his faith did fail, and when he had
turned again and did strengthen his brethren. "I have prayed
for you" is the prayer of Christ moving in all our inarticulate
groans and gladness. It is the foundation of all our intercession; we can bring all those of concern to us into its flow.
When we have reached the limits of what we can do and say
for a friend and he goes into an empty house, an empty room,
an empty bed, we can pray him into the all-embracing "I have
prayed for you." Alan Paton gives flesh to the spirit of our
prayer in the form of a letter to his son at the time of his
confirmation.

I see my son is wearing long trousers, I tremble at this:
I see he goes forward confidently, he does not know so fully his
own gentleness.
Go forward, eager and reverent child, see here I begin to take my
hands away from you.
I shall see you walk careless on the edges of the precipice, but if
you wish you shall hear no word come out of me;
My whole soul will be sick with apprehension, but I shall not
disobey you.
Life sees you coming, she sees you come with assurance towards
her,
She lies in wait for you, she cannot but hurt you;
Go forward, go forward, I hold the bandages and ointments ready,
And if you would go elsewhere and lie alone with your wounds,
why I shall not intrude upon you,
If you would seek the help of some other person, I shall not come
forcing myself upon you.
If you should fall into sin, innocent one, that is the way of this
pilgrimage;
Struggle against it, not for one fraction of a moment concede its
dominion.
It will occasion you grief and sorrow, it will torment you
But hate not God, nor turn from Him in shame or self-reproach;
He has seen many such, His compassion is as great as His Crea-
tion.
Be tempted and fall and return, return and be tempted and fall,
A thousand times and a thousand, even to a thousand thousand,
For out of this tribulation there comes a peace, deep in the soul
and surer than any dream.[42]

So we pray for one another, so God prays for us all.

   Prayer is the confrontation with a brother in the presence
of Christ where we know that no other man, even this
brother, is as sinful as we are. It is the acknowledgment that
whenever I regard my brother as a greater sinner than myself,
I am both blind and unforgiven. Prayer for another acknowledges that the only way to forgiveness is through my brother,
that I cannot go to God for pardon save through my brother

who is alienated from me. We may only go together, and this
is the depth of praying for our enemies (Matt. 5:44-45).
Bonhoeffer counsels us in our prayer to bear the freedom of
our brother. "The freedom of the other person includes all
that we mean by a person's nature, individuality, endowment.
It also includes his weaknesses and oddities which are such a
trial to our patience, everything that produces frictions, conflicts and collisions among us. To bear the burden of the other
person means involvement with the created reality of the
other, to accept and affirm it, and in bearing with it, to break
through to the point where we take joy in it."[43] Intercession
means to pray toward reconciliation, confident that He who
began a good work in us will bring it to completion on the day
of Christ (Phil. 1:6). So by faith the future becomes the
present.

We offer the present to God. We offer ourselves, our
friends and our enemies as we now are and our world as it
now is, everything, with thanksgiving. As Heschel says, "We
do not sacrifice. We are the sacrifice!"[44] We offer ourselves
as a living sacrifice (Rom. 12:1-2). The woman who danced
in our chancel during the Arts Festival said in conversation,
"I try to teach my students the difference between trying to be
the best, and to give one's best. It is the difference between
self-glorification and glorifying God. For me, my art, my
dancing, is an offering, a gift."[45] We offer ourselves just as
we are, without one plea, or with many pleas.

In the play The Devils, Grandier, a Libertine priest on trial
for the charge of demon possession, confesses to Father
Ambrose in his prison cell, "I can't pray. I can't give myself to
God, my unworthy self. I have lived by the senses." Ambrose
says to him tenderly, "Then die by the senses. Give God your
pain, your fear, your physical needs.[46] Whenever we give
God our real suffering selves, we are praying, we are committing ourselves and our world into the Father's hands. It is
always what we ought to do; it is always what we can do.

NOTES

CHAPTER I   The Pietist–Secularist Controversy in the Congregation

1. Edward Albee, *The Zoo Story* (New York: Coward-McCann, 1960).
2. James Kavanaugh, *A Modern Priest Looks at His Outdated Church* (New York Trident Press, 1967). Richard L. Rubenstein, *After Auschwitz* (Indianapolis: Bobbs-Merrill, 1966).
3. Edward Farley, *Requiem for a Lost Piety* (Philadelphia: Westminster Press, 1966), p. 17. (Piety is "that which unifies the specific interpretation of the Gospel.")
4. Paul van Buren, *The Secular Meaning of the Gospel* (New York: Macmillan, 1963), p. 18. See also: Ronald Gregor Smith, *Secular Christianity* (New York: Harper & Row, 1966).
5. John A. T. Robinson, *But That I Can't Believe* (London: Collins, Fontana Books, 1967), p. 76.
6. Robert McAfee Brown, *The Spirit of Protestantism* (New York: Oxford University Press, Galaxy Book, 1965), pp. 11-12.
7. Albert Camus, *The Fall* (New York: Random House, Vintage Book, 1956), p. 114.
8. Pierre Teilhard de Chardin, *Hymn of the Universe* (New York: Harper & Row, 1965), pp. 140-141.
9. Gunther Bornkamm, *Jesus of Nazareth* (New York: Harper & Row, 1960).
10. A. R. Vidler, *Essays in Liberality* (Naperville, Ill.: Alec R. Allenson, 1957), Chap. V. See also: Dietrich Bonhoeffer, *Letters and Papers from Prison* (London: SCM Press, 1953), pp. 168-169: "During the last year or so I have come to appreciate 'the worldliness' of Christianity as never before. . . . I don't mean the shallow this-worldliness of the enlightened, of the busy, the comfortable, or the lascivious. It's something much

more profound than that, something in which the knowledge of death and resurrection is ever present. . . . It means taking life in one's stride, with all its duties and problems, its successes and failures, its experiences and helplessness. It is in such a life that we throw ourselves utterly in the arms of God and participate in his sufferings in the world and watch with Christ in Gethsemane. That is faith. . . . and that is what makes a man and a Christian."

11. The *Christian Century* spoofed the just-plain-worldliness jag in vogue these days by suggesting guidelines for would-be-authors of books on secular Christianity (such as this one!). One bit of advice: "Briefly review the earlier interpretations of Dietrich Bonhoeffer and show how none of them has gone far enough. It is important to show that you are able to go further. Be autobiographical: I am a secular man. I know that God is dead. All around me people are reading *Playboy*, going boating on Sunday and making decisions in the laboratory without having God figure in their activities at all. As soon as Christians get the last little bit of religion out of their systems they can join the world and be as happy and sunny and agnostic as all the secular men who obviously have *Got It Made*." (Pen-Ultimate, "Wanted: Daring Manuscripts," *Christian Century*, August 18, 1965, p. 1023.) In a secular era, the Church is tempted to be vogue on the outside and vague on the inside.

12. John A. T. Robinson, *Honest to God* (London: SCM Press, 1963), p. 84.

13. Otherworldly holiness is a perversion of biblical holiness in which we wrongly separate ourselves from "the world," regarding others who think or behave differently as less holy than we, condemning them and feeling holier-than-thou. An example of this spurious otherworldly holiness appeared in a journalist's newspaper column in which he was critical of clergymen who became involved in such worldly matters as marches and demonstrations. At the end of the column was a statement which, in my judgment, reveals a basic misunderstanding of what it means, in biblical terms, to follow Jesus: "Many clergymen seem to have lost the halo of God's light and to have been plunged into the darkness of life itself." (David Lawrence, "Is the Clergyman Changing His Role," *U. S. News and World Report*, April 19, 1965, p. 116.) That is just what happened to Jesus. That is just what should happen to us. That is just what the Cross is all about. We have to let the phony holier-than-thou halo go and

plunge into the darkness of man's sin and suffering, where the Cross is plunged, and where Christ is calling us to follow him.

14. Harvey Cox, *The Secular City* (New York: Macmillan, 1965), pp. 2-3.

15. *Ibid.*, pp. 21-30.

16. Werner and Lotte Pelz, *God Is No More* (Philadelphia: J. B. Lippincott, 1964), pp. 40-41. A striking description of Jesus' call to commitment is found here. "The words of Jesus . . . lure us into adventurous committal by means of a highly dangerous promise: 'Follow me . . . and you shall see the heavens open . . . more than any lover has yet dared to promise. They call us into the reckless acceptance of ever shifting and changing human relationships, into unreserved committal to the explosive, a-moral, creative experience of love, friendship, and companionship, into our adolescent dream of life, as into our true life.' 'Sell all you have, give it away and come and follow me, if you want eternal life.' I am convinced that the original 'follow me' of Jesus is precisely such a call into reckless, unpremeditated friendship, for the sake of which a man is asked to leave father and mother and even his wife, if she be not the better friend. It is this call which makes Jesus unique among the great teachers. Unlike Buddha or Socrates he does not primarily offer wisdom, but simply himself. . . . the disciples who first heard the call, were not called into a mystical relationship with a divine being, but into a very earthy and risky one with a homeless vagrant who promised them that in their mutual love they would find all they had ever hoped for."

17. McLandlish Phillips, "A 'School Without Walls' Is Opened in Flushing," *New York Times*, September 21, 1966, p. 41M. "It is known as an 'open space' school. . . . It has few interior walls, and it just about does away with corridors and doors inside. It was designed so that 'instead of the kids fitting the school, the school fits the kids.' . . . All the furniture is movable, permitting flexibility and innovation in adapting the 7,850 square foot circular area to varying needs. It is a bit like a big living room. . . . 'People crave openness.' . . ." The article is suggestive not only for those seeking to design "open-space" church buildings without walls, but also as a parable of the style of life of a secular congregation. See also: Howard Moody, "Toward a Religionless Church for a Secular World," *Renewal* (May, 1965), p. 8; published by the Chicago Missionary Society, Chicago, Ill.

18. Horton Davies, "The Puritan and Pietist Traditions of Protestant

Spirituality," *Worship*, Vol. 39. No. 10, December, 1965 (Collegeville, Minnesota: Liturgical Press), pp. 597ff.

19. George Trevelyan, *English Social History* (London: Longmans, Green, 1942), p. 362. "The greatest and most justly famous of the manifestations of 'methodism' was the revivalist preaching of the Wesleys and Whitefield, which deeply moved a vast mass of human beings hitherto neglected by Church and State. And fortunately John Wesley's genius lay not only in his power as a revivalist preacher but in his gifts as an organizer. By forming his converts into permanent congregations he began a new chapter in the religious, social, and educational history of the working class. The Coincidence in time of Wesley and the Industrial Revolution had profound effects upon England for generations to come."

20. John Harmon, "Life Together in the City," *Catholic World*, August, 1965 (The Paulist Fathers), p. 325.

CHAPTER II   Secular Evangelism: *Covenant House*

1. New York *Times*, April 20, 1967, p. 1. See also Julius Horwitz, "The Arithmetic of Delinquency," New York Times *Magazine*, January 31, 1965, p. 12. (A shocking account of the inevitability of delinquency, statistically predictable, in slum areas.)

2. Thomas Wiesser (ed.), *Planning for Mission* (New York: U. S. Conference for World Council of Churches, 1966), pp. 201-202. ". . . the call is for a complete mental somersault out of our ingrained habit of inclusive, church-centered thinking towards an audacious preparedness for the dispersion of the body of Christians in two's and three's committed to an 'Abrahamitic' venture into the *terra incognito* of the twentieth century secular structures."

3. George W. Webber, *The Congregation in Mission* (Nashville: Abingdon Press, 1964), p. 169.

4. John 21:4; John 20:14. John 20:20 (Note: *then* (my italics), i.e.: when Jesus showed them his hands and his side, the disciples were glad when they saw the Lord. The implication is that at first they did not recognize him.); Luke 24:16.

5. H. Richard Niebuhr, *The Purpose of the Church and Its Ministry* (New York: Harper & Row, 1956), p. 27.

6. Dietrich Bonhoeffer, *Life Together* (New York: Harper & Row, 1954), p. 104.

7. For more information, write Chaplain Robert L. Dutton, P.O. Box 43, Norfolk, Mass. 02056.
8. Statement made by Al Carmines, Associate Minister, Judson Church, New York City.
9. Joan Hemenway, "Covenant House in Philadelphia," *Christian Century*, October 27, 1965, p. 1316.
10. Cf. Luke 14:12-22. Rough translation for us: Woe to those who neither hold such banquets nor go to them when invited. Pentecost parties do seem to be the Holy Spirit's specialty (Acts 2:42).

CHAPTER III   Secular Evangelism: *The Congregation Without Walls*

1. Hendrikus Berkhof, "The Church's Calling to Witness and to Service," *Christian Century*, October 16, 1957, p. 227.
2. Elizabeth O'Connor, *Journey Inward, Journey Outward* (New York: Harper & Row, 1968).
3. Paul W. Pruyser, "Joy," *Journal of Pastoral Care*, June 1966, Vol. XX, pp. 90-94.
4. Sydney Carter, "Lord of the Dance" (traditional English tune adapted by S. Carter), *Risk—New Hymns for a New Day*, Vol. II, No. 3 (Geneva: World Council of Churches, 1966), pp. 31-33.

1. I danced in the morning when the world was begun,
   And I danced in the moon and the stars and the sun,
   And I came down from heaven and I danced on the earth,
   At Bethlehem I had my birth.
       Chorus: Dance, then, wherever you may be;
                   I am the Lord of the Dance, said He.
                   And I'll lead you all wherever you may be,
                   And I'll lead you all in the Dance said He.

2. I danced for the scribe and the pharisee,
   But they would not dance and they wouldn't follow me,
   I danced for the fishermen, for James and John;
   They came with me and the dance went on. (*Chorus*)

3. I danced on the Sabbath and I cured the lame,
   The holy people said it was a shame
   They whipped and they stripped and they hung me high
   And they left me there on a Cross to die. (*Chorus*)

4. I danced on a Friday when the sky turned black;
   It's hard to dance with the devil on your back;
   They buried my body and they thought I'd gone,
   But I am the Dance and I still go on. (*Chorus*)

5. They cut me down and I leap up high;
   I am the life that'll never, never die.
   I'll live in you if you'll live in me;
   I am the Lord of the Dance, said He. (*Chorus*)

5. John Carr, pastor of the Church of the Saviour, Indianapolis, Indiana: "I am reminded of a *Saturday Review* cartoon which perfectly caught the dangerous if blessed messiness involved in walls coming tumbling down. It pictured an ancient walled city (Jericho), with several trumpeters sitting on horses, lined up next to the walls, trumpets poised to blow. One of the trumpeters is asking another, 'Say which way are those walls going to come tumbling down?'"
6. H. Richard Niebuhr, *The Responsible Self* (New York: Harper & Row, 1963), 177.

CHAPTER IV   Secular Covenant: *The Covenant Group*

1. Joan Hemenway, "Covenant House in Philadelphia," *Christian Century*, October 27, 1965, pp. 1316-1317.
2. Joan Hemenway, "Covenant House, Inc.," paper prepared for "Missions 224" class at Union Theological Seminary, September, 1966.
3. *Ibid.*
4. Dietrich Bonhoeffer, *Life Together* (New York: Harper & Row, 1954), pp. 16-101. Quotation from p. 101.
5. Letty M. Russell, *Christian Education in Mission* (Philadelphia: Westminster Press, 1967), p. 61.
6. Albert Camus, quoted by Norman Cousins in editorial "Confrontation," *Saturday Review*, March 25, 1961, p. 32.

CHAPTER V   Secular Covenant: *The Congregation with Roots*

1. The sacrament of Baptism should be administered in the context of congregational worship whenever possible. A private ceremony is like having a birthday party without the family being present to celebrate. Baptism is a *congregational* event, expressed in the

congregational pledge of responsibility for the Christian education of the person being baptized.

The Congregational Response: "We rejoice to receive these
persons into the family of Christ. We pledge ourselves as their
friends and counselors to guide them by our precept and example that they may grow in knowledge and love of God according to the measure of the stature of the fullness of Christ.
Amen."

There are occasions, of course, when a private family celebration may be appropriate; but the norm is public celebration.

2. Robert A. Raines, *New Life in the Church* (New York: Harper
& Row, 1961). Raines, *Reshaping the Christian Life* (New
York: Harper & Row, 1964).

3. Koinonia groups are thoroughly described in the books cited in
note 2, above.

4. Letty Russell, *Christian Education in Mission* (Philadelphia:
Westminster Press, 1967), pp. 59-73.

5. Paul Chapman, "Training for Ecumenical Dialogue," a talk
given at the Inaugural Meeting of the North American Academy
of Ecumenism, Chicago, Ill., June, 1967.

6. Helmut Thieleke, *The Waiting Father* (New York: Harper &
Row, 1959).

7. Charles Mercer, "Thoughts on Relocation," prepared for *MAP*,
December 7, 1964.

8. After the North Philadelphia riots in 1964, the Mayor of the
city proposed adding one thousand more policemen to the police
force as the chief means of dealing with riots, and "controlling"
the ghetto where they had broken out. Jerry Rardin reminded
us at the time of T. S. Eliot's pertinent words, "Can you keep
the city that the Lord keeps not with you? A thousand policemen directing the traffic cannot tell you why you come or where
you go" (T. S. Eliot, "Choruses from the Rock", *The Complete Poems and Plays* [New York: Harcourt, Brace, and World,
1930-52], p. 103). No, nor can they cure the ghetto of its
festering wounds, or the city of its sickness.

9. How much the litany, and the reading of it, means to the laymen who do the reading is indicated by the fact that more than
one of them has added (unconsciously) the word "very" to the
third line of the Leader, thus, "caring for the (very) least of
thy children."

10. Paul W. Pruyser, "Joy," *Journal of Pastoral Care,* June 1966, Vol. XX, pp. 90-94.
11. J. C. Hoekendijk, *The Church Inside Out* (Philadelphia: Westminster Press, 1964).

CHAPTER VI Secular Prayer

1. Abraham J. Heschel, *Man's Quest for God* (New York: Charles Scribner's Sons, 1954), p. 61.
2. William Hamilton and Thomas J. J. Altizer, *Radical Theology and the Death of God* (Indianapolis: Bobbs-Merrill Co., 1966), pp. 28, 31, 47, 50. It is not clear to me whether Hamilton is inviting us to wait for the *living* God, or whether the term "waiting" is a hopeful expression of a theology of despair.
3. Albert Camus, *The Plague* (New York: Random House, Modern Library, 1948), pp. 117-118.
4. Paul van Buren, *The Secular Meaning of the Gospel* (New York: Macmillan, 1963), p. 189.
5. Morris West, *The Shoes of the Fisherman* (New York: Morrow, 1963), p. 60.
6. Gunther Bornkamm, *Jesus of Nazareth* (New York: Harper & Row, 1960), p. 128. See also David L. Edwards, *The Honest to God Debate* (Philadelphia: Westminster Press, 1963), p. 262. "I do not pray to the ground of my being. I pray to God as Father. Prayer, for the Christian, is the opening of one's self to that utterly gracious personal reality which Jesus could only address as 'Abba Father!' " (John A. T. Robinson)
7. Martin Buber, *I and Thou* (New York: Charles Scribner's Sons, 1958), pp. 135-136. "The description of God as a Person is indispensable for everyone who like myself means by God not a principle . . . not an idea: but him who enters into direct relation with us men in creative, revealing and redeeming acts, and thus makes it possible for us to enter into a direct relation with him. . . . The concept of personal being is indeed completely incapable of declaring what God's essential being is, but it is both permitted and necessary to say that God is also a Person . . . the Absolute Person, i.e. the Person who cannot be limited."
8. Paul Tillich, *Systematic Theology* (Chicago: University of Chicago Press, 1951), Vol. I, p. 267.
9. John Coburn, "Contemporary Non-Catholic Spirituality and the Guidance of Souls," *Worship,* December, 1965, p. 60. Also

available separately as *Protestants and Catholics on the Spiritual Life*, edited by Michael Marx, O.S.B. (Collegeville, Minn.: Liturgical Press, 1965).

10. Abraham J. Heschel, *Man's Quest for God*, p. 71.

11. Quoted in Robert A. Raines, *Creative Brooding* (New York: Macmillan, 1966), Introduction.

12. Horton Davies, Henry W. Putnam Professor of the History of Christianity at Princeton University. A phrase of his used in conversation.

13. Karl Barth, see his comment quoted on p. 103.

14. John A. T. Robinson, *Honest to God* (London: SCM Press, 1963), p. 103.

15. Pierre Teilhard de Chardin, *Hymn of the Universe* (New York: Harper & Row, 1965), p. 34. "Christ of glory, hidden power stirring in the heart of matter. . . ."

16. Malcolm Boyd, *Are You Running with Me, Jesus?* (New York: Holt, Rinehart and Winston, 1965), p. 11.

17. *Ibid.* pp. 12, 15, 60, 17, 90, 89.

18. Michel Quoist, *Prayers* (New York: Sheed and Ward, 1963), pp. v-vi.

19. Exod. 34:14-16; Matt. 28:20. Here is the "ambulatory" God, the wandering God of Exodus, who dwelt incognito in a cloud by day and fire by night, whose presence went with his people.

20. From a conversation between John Ciardi and Ted Loder.

21. Herb Gardner, *A Thousand Clowns* (1961, 1962, by Herb Gardner and Irwin A. Cantor, Trustee, N.Y.).

22. John Ruskin, *Modern Painters*, Vol. III, Part IV, Chap. 16, Section 28. "The greatest thing a human soul ever does in this world is to see something, and then to tell what it saw in a plain way. Hundreds of people can talk for one who can think, but thousands can think for one who can see. To see clearly is poetry, prophecy, and religion all in one."

23. Nikos Kazantzakes, *Zorba, the Greek* (New York: Simon & Schuster, 1959).

25. Garmen Bernow de Basztold, *Prayers from the Ark* (New York: Viking Press, 1962), p. 59.

26. Fyodor Dostoevski, *The Brothers Karamazov* (New York: Random House Modern Library), p. 126.

27. Michel Quoist, *Prayers* (New York: Sheed and Ward, 1963), p. 145.

28. Related by William Coffin in a sermon.

29. Søren Kierkegaard, *Works of Love*, trans. Howard and Edna Hong (New York: Harper Torchbooks, 1962), translator's introduction, p. 12, note. 2.

30. Martin Buber, *I and Thou* (New York: Charles Scribner's Sons, 1958), p. 64.

31. Abraham J. Heschel, *Man's Quest for God*, pp. 59-64. (A beautiful description of what it means to stand before God.)

32. Dietrich Bonhoeffer, *Life Together* (New York: Harper & Row, 1954), p. 77. "Let him who cannot be alone beware of community."

33. Abraham J. Heschel, *Man's Quest for God*, p. 64.

34. From a conversation with Professor Jean LeClerq, O.S.B., Abbaye Saint-Maurice, Clervaux, Luxembourg.

35. Abraham J. Heschel, *Man's Quest for God*, pp. 27-30.

36. John Ciardi, from a lecture delivered at the 1967 Arts Festival of the First Methodist Church of Germantown, Philadelphia.

37. From a conversation with Father Thomas Hopco, St. John the Baptist Church, Hoyt St., Warren, Ohio.

38. From a conversation with Professor Jean LeClerq, O.S.B., Abbaye Saint-Maurice, Clervaux, Luxembourg.

39. Ecclesiastes; Albert Camus, *The Plague*, pp. 117-118; Jesus: Mark 15:34.

40. Cf. Thomas Kelly, *A Testament of Devotion* (New York: Harper & Row, 1941), p. 109. Kelly's phrase: "We cannot die on every cross, nor are we expected to."

41. Dietrich Bonhoeffer, *Letters and Papers from Prison* (London: SCM Press, 1953), pp. 91-92.

42. Alan Paton, "Meditation for a Young Boy Confirmed," *Christian Century*, 1954.

43. Dietrich Bonhoeffer, *Life Together*, p. 101.

44. Abraham J. Heschel, *Man's Quest for God*, p. 71.

45. From a conversation with Audrey Gulov Bookspan, Dancing Philosopher, resident of Philadelphia, Pa.

46. John Osborne, *The Devils*.

SCRIPTURE INDEX